W9-CFL-249

# *50 Cars*
## TO
## DRIVE

*The first great Ferrari road car, the 1950 type 166 MM, car No. 20 on our list*

# TO DRIVE

**DENNIS ADLER**

*with*

JAY LENO | CARROLL SHELBY | SIR STIRLING MOSS | BOB BONDURANT
DAN GURNEY | SAM MOSES | BRUCE MEYER | LUIGI CHINETTI JR.

THE LYONS PRESS
Guilford, Connecticut
An Imprint of The Globe Pequot Press

The Lyons Press is an imprint of The Globe Pequot Press.

On the cover:
The most coveted of our 50 cars to drive, a 1957 Ferrari Testa Rossa.
Photo by Dennis Adler from the Bruce Meyer collection
All photos courtesy of Dennis Adler unless otherwise noted.

Text design by Casey Shain

Library of Congress Cataloging-in-Publication Data
Adler, Dennis, 1948-
50 cars to drive / by Dennis Adler
p.cm.
ISBN 978-1-59921-230-2
1. Automobiles—History. 2. Automobiles—Collectors and collecting. I. Title. II. Title: Fifty cars to drive.
TL15.A342 2008
629.222—dc22
2007049951

Printed in China

10 9 8 7 6 5 4 3 2 1

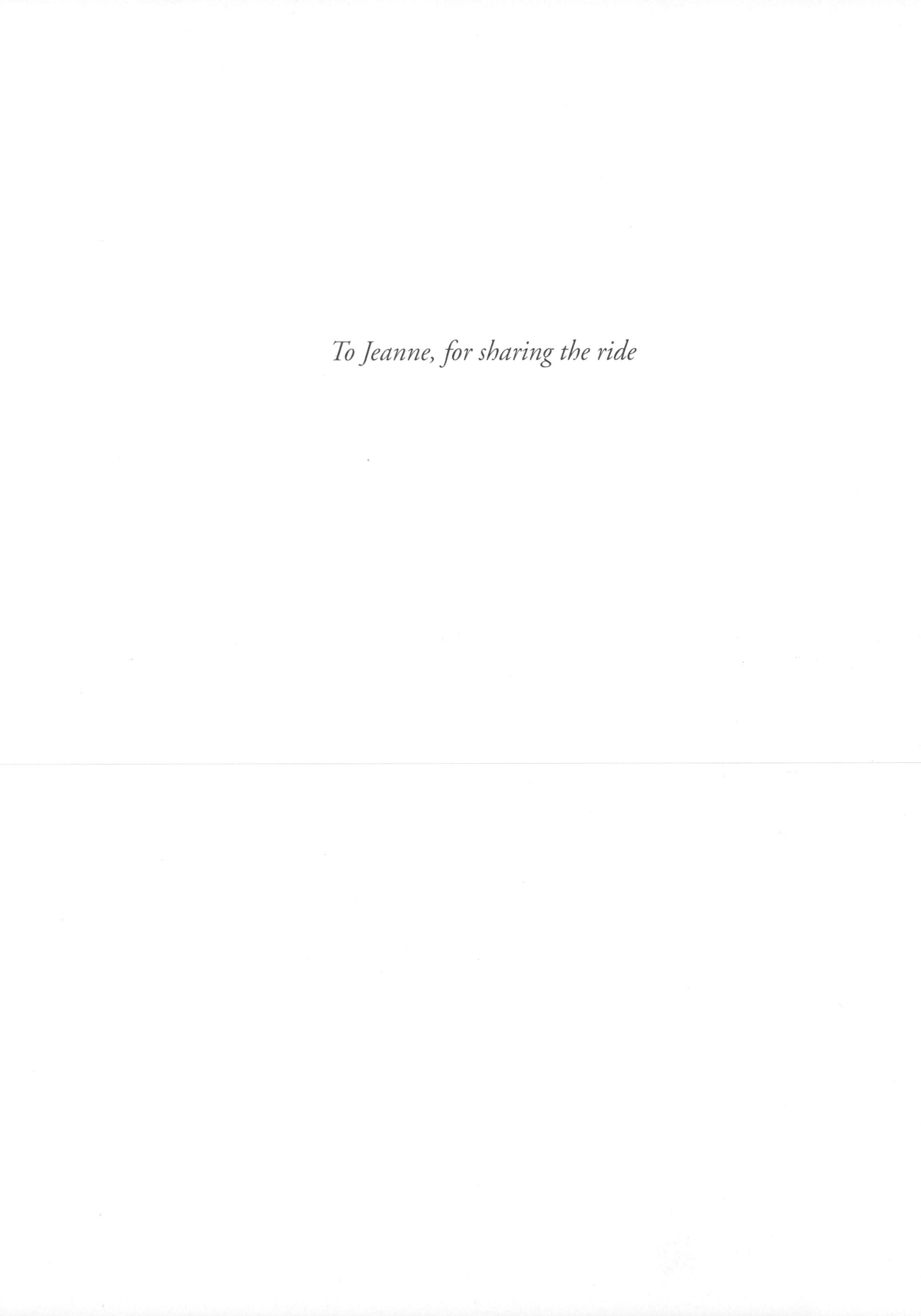

*To Jeanne, for sharing the ride*

# Contents

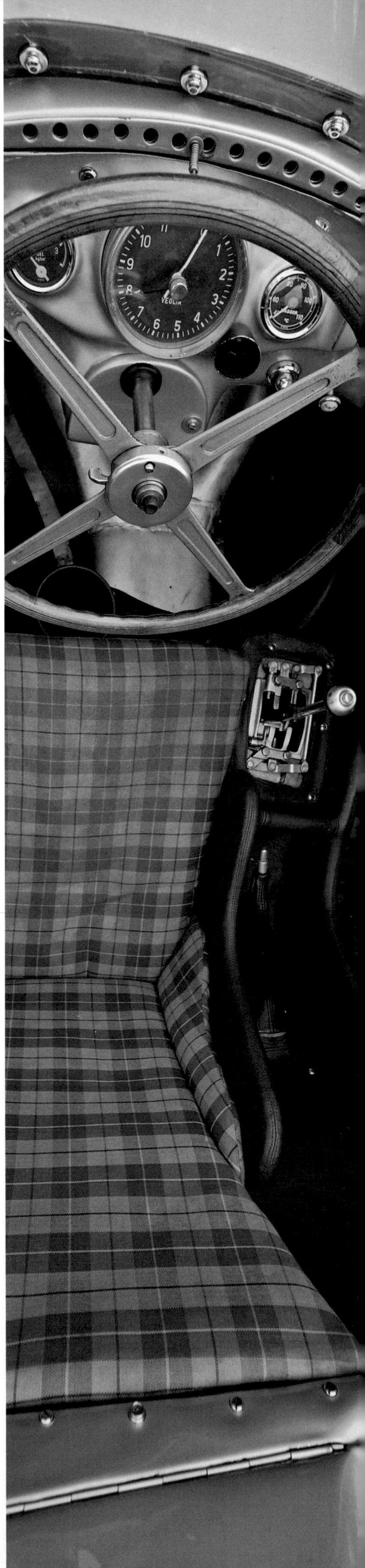

PT-97 15

# *Introduction*

*This book is based on a simple principle: that there are cars, and then there are* cars. *The latter are more than mere transportation or grocery-getters; they are, as the old automotive journalist's cliché goes, "greater than the sum of their parts." Driving them becomes a life's experience. Every car in this book is worth seeking out, if only to get a few minutes behind the wheel. Nothing is impossible.*

—DENNIS ADLER

**EXCITING CARS.** Exciting cars come from every era in automotive history; even a car that is more than a century old can be the thrill of a lifetime to drive. Consider sitting behind the tiller of an 1886 Benz three-wheeler—the first patented motor vehicle—or dashing down the road in a 1913 Mercer Raceabout—the Corvette Z06 of its day. Who wouldn't want to get behind the wheel of a multi-million dollar 1930s Bugatti Royale, and the next day a brand-new 2007 Bugatti Veyron?

Heritage and history play a great role in *50 Cars To Drive*. Spanning more than 100 years of motoring, every automobile in this tale of mechanical and stylistic achievement bears a historical imperative, anything from being the first of its kind to the best of its time, in its time. If you love Mercedes-Benz, then you have to catch a stint behind the wheel of Rudolf Uhlenhaut's 1955 300 SLR Gullwing Coupe or take a ride around Italy's historic Mille Miglia road course with Sir Stirling Moss and his championship 300 SLR Roadster. Then top off your day by driving the all-new Mercedes-Benz SLR McLaren.

Going fast isn't the only joy of motoring. Imagine yourself behind the tiller of the first automobile, an 1886 Benz Motorwagen, or silently motoring down Michigan Avenue in a 1918 Detroit Electric.

Think American and you have to pick cars by decades. For better than half of the twentieth century Detroit was the automotive capital of the world. What was the hottest ride of the late 1910s and Roaring Twenties? You'd be surprised to find out it might have been a Packard! In the 1930s it was a supercharged Duesenberg Boattail Speedster—the mightiest American motorcar. How about driving a V16 Cadillac Aero-Dynamic Coupe, one of the most historically significant designs of the 1930s? And if all your stars are aligned, you might get behind the wheel of Ab Jenkins' Mormon Meteor and take it for a spin on the Bonneville Salt Flats before sundown.

From the 1950s, there are a handful of great American cars worth getting into. How about one of those rare and almost impossible to find 1950s GM Motorama Dream Cars or a Chrysler Turbine?

*Car No. 38 is a legend in the automotive world, the Hispano-Suiza J-12.*

From the rare to the unimaginable, these are cars that have become much more than a means of getting from one place to another; they have become a part of our history and more importantly, our culture. This is a book about 50 cars that could change your entire perception of the automobile with one trip around the block.

## THE PANEL

Legendary racecar drivers, historians, and collectors—people who have lived and breathed motorcars for most of their lives—comprise our panel of automotive authorities.

**AUTHOR DENNIS ADLER:** An award-winning automotive historian, Dennis Adler is the editorial director of *Car Collector* magazine. During his 30-plus years as an author he has written more than 30 books, the most recent of which include *Daimler & Benz—The Complete History*, published in 2006 by HarperCollins, and *Ferrari—The Road From Maranello*, published in 2006 by Random House. For nearly 25 years, Mr. Adler was also the senior contributing editor for the Mercedes-Benz Club of America publication *The Star*. With more than 5,000 articles and photographs published, he is regarded as one of the leading authorities on American classic cars and the history of Mercedes-Benz.

**JAY LENO:** America's ambassador to the automotive world, *Tonight Show* host Jay Leno is not only a collector but an authority on American and European cars spanning more than a century of production. Jay has often said he gets as much pleasure out of working on his cars as he does driving them and is just as capable of tearing down a Blower Bentley as he is tearing around in it. Jay's automotive tastes span the entire history of the automobile, which is reflected in his own car collection.

**CARROLL SHELBY:** Perhaps the most recognizable name in American motoring history, Carroll began his career as a racecar driver in the 1950s. After a heart condition forced him from behind the wheel, he became the most prolific manufacturer of muscle cars in America. After more than 45 years in the automotive business, he is still going strong with the latest renditions of the Shelby Cobra and Shelby Mustangs. Shelby's automotive legacy includes the 289 and 427 Cobras, the Shelby Daytona Cobra, GT40 Mk IV (1967 Le Mans winner), and Shelby Mustang GT350 and GT500.

**SIR STIRLING MOSS:** The list of racing drivers that have been knighted by the Queen of England is short, to say the least, and no one is more renowned for his career in motorsports than Sir Stirling, a man who raced down the wind on every continent while competing in 495 motorsport events, driving 84 different cars, reaching the finishing line in 366 races, and winning 222 of them. He missed the World Champion's title by a hair's breadth several times, clinching the runner-up position four times between 1955 and 1958, three times behind the great Juan Manuel Fangio and once, in 1958, behind his compatriot Mike Hawthorn. His record of success also boasts 16 pole positions and a total of 19 fastest laps in World Championship races, plus his unforgettable victory in the 1955 Mille Miglia.

**BOB BONDURANT:** With a lifelong passion for motorcycle racing, by age 18 Bob was campaigning an Indian Scout motorcycle on the local dirt ovals around Los Angeles and soon moved to sports cars, sitting behind the wheel of a Morgan in 1956. His racing career began to soar three years later: Driving a Corvette in the Southern California region, Bob captured the West Coast "B" Production Championship and the Corvette Driver of the Year Award. In 1963, he

*One of the greatest postwar MG models, the MGA Twin Cam was both roadcar and racecar. It is No. 41 on our list.*

joined the team of Carroll Shelby and Ford Cobras in Europe, going on to win numerous races and a chance to compete in the 1964 World GT Championship. Paired with Dan Gurney, Bob won the GT Category overall and placed 4th in a Cobra Daytona Coupe at Le Mans. He remained in Europe in 1965 and drove to win seven out of 10 races, earning him the World Manufacturers' Championship for the United States behind the wheel of a Shelby Cobra. That honor would put Bob in Formula One for Ferrari at the Watkins Glen Grand Prix. In 1966, Bob continued with Ferrari, driving in the World Manufacturers' Championship for Dan Gurney's All American Racers Team. Today he owns and operates the most famous professional driving school in the country. Located in Phoenix, Arizona, the school maintains more than 200 race-prepared vehicles, sedans, and open wheel cars and is the largest facility of its kind in North America.

**DAN GURNEY:** Dan has had multiple careers as a racing driver, racecar manufacturer and team owner, and inventor. His racing career, which started with a Triumph TR2 in 1955, spanned 15 years. During that time he became the top road-racing star in America, as well as one of the most popular F1 Grand Prix drivers ever. Gurney etched himself a place in racing lore with exciting battles against drivers like Stirling Moss, Jimmy Clark, John Surtees, Jack Brabham, Graham Hill, Phil Hill, and many others on the classic road courses of the Nürburgring, the Targa Florio, and Monte Carlo. He remains the only U.S. citizen to win a Grand Prix in a car of his own construction in the 100-year history of F1 racing!

By the time he retired from active driving in 1970, Gurney had raced in 312 events in 20 countries with 51 different makes of cars, winning 51 races and finishing on the podium an additional 47 times. Among his most important victories: seven Formula One races (four Grand Prix World Championship events), seven Indy Car races, five NASCAR Winston Cup stock car races (all 500-mile races in Riverside, California), and two 2nd place finishes at the Indianapolis 500. Additionally, he captured wins in Trans-Am, Can-Am, and sports car races including the endurance classics at the Nürburgring, Daytona, Sebring, and Le Mans. He claimed 42 career pole positions and started on the front row of the grid an additional and astonishing 58 times! This versatile and winning record made Dan the first driver ever to win races in the four major categories of motorsports: Grand Prix, Indy Car, NASCAR, and Sports Car. To this day he is one of only two drivers in history (the other being Mario Andretti) ever to win the "quadruple crown" of racing.

**SAM MOSES:** Author, racecar driver, and motorsports journalist Sam Moses began his writing career covering Grand Prix motorcycle racing in Europe. He was a staff writer for *Sports Illustrated* for 17 years, covering the motorsports beat. His memorable book, *Fast Guys, Rich Guys and Idiots*, provided a sharp and vivid gaze through the windscreen of semi-pro sports car racing. The book, published by Bison Books, was voted by the *Wall Street Journal* as "one the five best books on motor racing." As deputy editor at *AutoWeek*, he wrote high-performance road and racing car reviews. In 1998 he received automotive journalism's prestigious Ken Purdy Award. More recently, he was creative director of a website covering the Mount Everest climbing season. His most recent book is the World War II adventure *At All Costs*, published by Random House.

**BRUCE MEYER:** A renowned collector of historic winning racecars from LeMans to Indy to Bonneville, Bruce is the founding chairman of the Petersen Automotive Museum in Los Angeles, California. A car guy's car guy, known and respected by all in the industry, he serves on the board of the Nethercutt Collection and the steering committees of the Pebble Beach Concours d'Elegance and the Harold E. LeMay Museum in Tacoma, Washington. He received the Meguiar's Award for the Collector Car Person of the Year, the Automotive Icon Award by the Petersen Automotive Museum, and is a member of the Dry Lakes Hall of Fame for his tireless work and promotion of historic hot-rodding. From Duesenbergs to Dragsters, from Cobras to Corvettes, from Indians to Indy cars—the best are represented in his stunning collection, which has won multiple awards at Pebble Beach and Concours from coast to coast.

He began his collection in 1964 with a 300 SL Gullwing and has had extensive experience piloting the best of the best worldwide. He has participated in the historic Italian Mille Miglia, the French Tour Auto, and the English Goodwood Festival of Speed, as well as all the important U.S. rallies . . . from the Colorado Grand to the Arizona Copperstate.

While his first passion is classic and postwar cars, like his sporty Model J Duesenberg, Porsche 356 speedster, Mercedes-Benz 300 SL Gullwing, and treasured 300Sc cabriolet (which was originally owned by Clark Gable), Bruce is also a hot-rod preservationist and historian, finding and restoring vintage examples from the 1950s, like the Pierson Brothers Bonneville competition coupe, which is part of his collection. "Hot rods are one of the purest American art forms," says the man who convinced the Pebble Beach Concours d'Elegance to create a hot-rod class in 1997.

**LUIGI CHINETTI JR.:** Former racecar driver (Le Mans class winner in 1971 driving a Ferrari 365 GTB/4), constructor, and team owner (North American Racing Team N.A.R.T.), Luigi has been a consummate sports car enthusiast his entire life. His father, Luigi Chinetti Sr., was the driving force (quite literally) behind the establishment of Ferrari S.p.A. after World War II.

He began his career in the late 1960s, racing for his father's North American Racing Team, the name for which, as Luigi explains, his father conceived of while stuck in traffic behind a North American Van Lines moving truck! N.A.R.T. became the acronym for Ferrari racing in America in the 1960s and 1970s. In addition to racing, Luigi Jr. was also a designer. Among the concepts to his credit is one of the rarest of all Ferraris, the 275 GTS/4 N.A.R.T. Spyder, which was sold exclusively by Chinetti Motors in Greenwich, Connecticut. A frequent class judge at Concours d'Elegance throughout the U.S. and Europe, Luigi also has a fine collection of Ferrari sports and racing cars. ◆

## *The Selection of Cars*

When you have a consensus of opinion, you have a car that everyone would like the opportunity to drive. Among the 100-plus vehicles nominated for *50 Cars To Drive*, the first 10 are regarded by this panel of experts as the most desirable. If you have driven even half of them, you are way ahead of the curve.

The next highest group of cars was selected individually by members of the panel, and the last 25 by the author based upon discussions over the years with individual owners and automotive museum staff and curators, as well as car-collecting trends over the last five years. What we have not done, however, is jump on a bandwagon of populist cars or follow traditional lines with cars that, as one collector said, are "as fundamental to automotive history as bacon and eggs is to breakfast." In other words, you will not find a Ford Model T, a 1965 Mustang, a 1970 Plymouth Hemi 'Cuda, a Corvette, a Thunderbird, or a Porsche 911 on our list. All very important cars, but not the experience we are seeking behind the wheel of our *50 Cars To Drive*.

**THE TOP 10**

1957 Ferrari Testa Rossa

Mercer Raceabout c. 1911–1913

Model SJ Duesenberg 1932–1937

1955 Mercedes-Benz 300 SLR

1961 Maserati Tipo 63/64

1955 Porsche 550 Spyder

1961 Ferrari 250 GT (SWB)
Short Wheelbase Berlinetta

1955 Jaguar D-Type

1939 Type 57C Bugatti

1937 Mercedes-Benz 540K

# *No.* 1

## 1957 FERRARI TESTA ROSSA

### *The Fiery Red Head*

**THE TESTA ROSSA IS REGARDED** as one of the most visceral sports car designs of all time. As functional as they were beautiful, the massive long nose and grille were designed to draw as much air as possible to the brakes and radiator. The projecting pontoon fenders of the first series housed the covered headlights, giving the car its striking appearance but not offering the aerodynamic advantages of the more enveloped body design introduced with the Series 2 model pictured.

As for the name, Testa Rossa was a paint color. To be exact, the red crackle paint used to cover the cylinder heads on the latest derivative of Gioacchino Colombo's high-revving V12 engine. Now with a swept volume of 3,000 cubic centimeters, the updated V12 made its debut in November 1957 under the hood of the first customer version of the 250 Testa Rossa, or red head, chassis 0710. West Coast Ferrari distributor and racecar driver John von Neumann purchased the silver Ferrari and sent the car from Italy on a circuitous trip to the 1957 Nassau Speed Week event via New York and Florida. Richie Ginther drove the car in Nassau, but in its first outing the 250 TR failed to finish. This was to be one of the very few times a 250 TR would not finish a race or, more often, win it. The factory team would win 10 of 20 races entered between 1958 and 1961 in World Sports Car Championship events and take the checkered flag at Le Mans in 1958, 1960, and 1961! In addition to the Testa Rossa's three wins at the Circuit de La Sarthe, privately entered 250 Testa Rossas finished 5th and 6th at Le Mans in 1958, making the 250 TR one of the most coveted sports cars in its time.

*The silver Series 2 Testa Rossa pictured, serial number 0672, is from the Bruce Meyer collection and began life as one of only two 1957 TRC 625 models. Now considered a TRC 625/250 TR, it was originally purchased by the West Coast Ferrari importer and racecar driver John von Neumann and campaigned in Southern California by von Neumann and Richie Ginther.*

The 250 TR's underpinnings were Ferrari's "conventional" bill of fare—an independent front suspension utilizing coil springs, live rear axle with semi elliptical springs, drum brakes, and a four-speed all-synchromesh gearbox located up front. Nothing was strikingly new about the driveline, only the increased power and the remarkable coachwork. That, however, was enough.

YOU DRIVE FROM THE RIGHT SEAT, THE MASSIVE GEARSHIFT TO YOUR LEFT. THE FERRARI V12 ROARS TO LIFE AND INSPIRES YOU TO EXPLORE THE CAR'S MAGNIFICENT SUSPENSION AND STEERING CAPABILITY. FROM BEHIND THE WHEEL THE OPEN COCKPIT GIVES YOU A VIEW ONLY RACE DRIVERS KNOW FIRST HAND. THE GEARBOX SHIFTS QUICKLY BUT DEMANDS A FIRM HAND. AS THE ROAD PASSES BY AND YOU TAKE THE CURVES, RACE DOWN THE STRAIGHTS, YOU UNDERSTAND WHY THIS IS ONE OF THE GREATEST SPORTS CARS EVER BUILT.

The earliest V12 models had featured distinctive coachwork by Carrozzeria Scaglietti in Modena, with bold, pontoon-style cutaway front fenders that left the massive oval grille standing alone. Later versions, like this example, chassis 0672, also once owned by John von Neumann, had the smoother fender line integrated into the grille. Neither 12-cylinder model, however, was the first Ferrari to bear the Testa Rossa name.

*Like all Ferrari race cars, the 250 TR was right-hand drive, with the shifter to the driver's left. The large central tachometer was the most important gauge on the panel with redline indicated at 6,500 rpm. Oil temperature, oil pressure, fuel level, and water temperature completed the instrumentation. There was no need for a speedometer. It was part of the pit crew's job to compute speed and lap times.*

10
20
30
40
50
60
70
80
90
100
0
JAEGER
GIRI x 100
Ferrari

The first Testa Rossas were powered by a four-cylinder Ferrari engine replete with the red crackle paint that had evolved from the factory's earlier 2-liter Mondial racecars. There were Series 1 (1954) and Series 2 Mondials (1955–1957), both with four-cylinder engines. The Mondials, unfortunately, proved no match for the new 2-liter Maseratis. The first Testa Rossas, the Tipo 500 TRC, built in 1956-57, had a swept volume of 2,000 cubic centimeters (versus

*Testa Rossa meant "Red Head." To be exact, the term refers to red crackle paint used to cover the cylinder heads on the latest derivative of Gioacchino Colombo's V12. The 250 TR was the ideal vehicle for reviving the seasoned V12, now at 2,953 cubic centimeters, with a phalanx of six twin-choke Webers and a stirring output of 300 horsepower. Top speed, dependent upon gearing, was more than 170 mph. (Bruce Meyer collection)*

1,984.8 cubic centimeters for the Mondial) and 190 horsepower, 30 more than the Series 1 and 20 more than the Series 2 Mondials. These first Testa Rossas won numerous international championship races, including the 2-liter class and second overall at Nassau in 1956, with a repeat in 1957, the 2-liter class in the 1957 Mille Miglia, the 1000km of Buenos Aires and Venezuela; and, in America, the 500 TRCs won top-place standing in class for the 1958 USAC Championship. The 2-liter Testa Rossa was discontinued in 1957, when Ferrari introduced the new 3-liter 250 TR model.

The 250 TR was the ideal vehicle for reviving Colombo's seasoned V12 engine, now at 2,953 cubic centimeters, with a phalanx of six twin-choke Webers and a stirring output of 300 horsepower. Top speed, dependent upon gearing, was more than 170 mph.

The frame for the 250 Testa Rossa was along lines similar to those of the 300 SL and Maserati Birdcage, utilizing a multi-tube configuration beneath the stunning coachwork of Sergio Scaglietti, who not only built the 250 TR but designed it as well. The *Gabbia* or "cage" (thus the Maserati's designation of Birdcage) was just that, a complete metal framework matching the contours of the outer skin, which was shaped on styling bucks and attached over the metal substructure.

This silver Series 2 is from the Bruce Meyer collection and began life as one of only two 1957 TRC 625 models, but it's now considered a TRC 625/250 TR because of the V12 engine living beneath its hood. John von Neumann and Richie Ginther originally raced it in Southern California. Von Neumann had one of the most important distributorships in the country, selling both Porsches and Ferraris, which was about as good as it got in the 1950s and 1960s. When Ferrari introduced the 500 TRC, it was von Neumann who convinced Enzo Ferrari to build two Testa Rossas with the 2.5-liter Le Mans engines, one of which was 0672. (The 625 was a four-cylinder, 2.5-liter Grand Prix engine, whereas the 250 TR was the new 3-liter V12 evolved from the original Colombo

*From the rear the sweep of the fenders shows the elegant lines penned by Scaglietti for the second Testa Rossa body style.*

design.) The first of the two 2.5-liter cars, it was shipped to the Auto Club of Mexico on March 24, 1956, where it remained in storage until von Neumann raced it at Avandaro in April. His first time behind the wheel of the Testa Rossa earned him a checkered flag. The car was then shipped back to Precision Motors in Los Angeles, where Richie Ginther and von Neumann campaigned 0672 for the balance of the 1957 racing season. Including victories at Santa Barbara, Salt Lake City, Pomona, Sacramento, and San Diego, the Testa Rossa and its two seasoned drivers won a total of 11 races by year's end.

The following year, 0672 was refitted with the new 250 Testa Rossa engine. Unfortunately, in 1958, the stars were not aligned for the 250 TR or for Ginther and von Neumann. Ginther won only a single race in Mexico City. Two years later he blew up the engine at the Times-Mirror Grand Prix at Riverside, and in 1961 von Neumann sold 0672 to fellow auto importer and race team owner Otto Zipper. The Testa Rossa began a new life with Zipper's team under the skilled hands of the legendary Ken Miles. The car's first outing for Otto Zipper's racing team was at Santa Barbara in May 1962, where Miles handily won the event. Later in the year, Miles blew up the engine at Pomona, and Zipper decided to retire the six-year-old racecar. By then John von Neumann had retired as well, not only from racing but from his import business after selling his Southern California region dealership to Volkswagen AG. As for 0672, it has been flawlessly restored and has a very nice home in Bruce Meyer's garage. ◆

ANTIQUE
2447
NEW HAMPSHIRE

# Mercer Raceabout c.1911–1913

## *Racing Down The Wind*

**CONSIDER THIS.** In 1911 almost any automobile built in America could be turned into a racecar by removing the bodywork. And in 1911 there wasn't much to remove. With very few exceptions, the majority of automobiles on the road were roadsters, phaetons, and tourers—the distinction being wheelbase length, the number of seats, and how many doors, or, in the case of roadsters, the lack thereof. Removing

IMAGINE A MOTORCYCLE WITH FOUR WHEELS. THE MERCER IS THAT VISCERAL. THE WIND RIPS PAST YOUR FACE, YES GOGGLES ARE REQUIRED, AND THE SENSATION OF "HANGING ON FOR DEAR LIFE" BECOMES YOUR CO-DRIVER. EVERYTHING IS IN THE OPEN, THE SHIFTER IS MOUNTED TO THE OUTSIDE OF THE FRAME, THE LITTLE THROTTLE PEDAL, FOOTBRAKE AND CLUTCH AGAINST THE FIREWALL.

fenders, body panels, and top bows required little more than a wrench and a few hand tools. In the case of the 1911 Mercer Raceabout, most of those body parts were never attached in the first place. This was one of America's first true sports cars, ready to go from dealer's floor to the racetrack with little more than a fine tuning of the

*There wasn't a lot to a Mercer Raceabout when it came to bodywork. There was little more to it than two seats, four fenders, a gas tank, and a hood over the engine, but that was enough to make this jaunty speedster one of the greatest cars of all time.*

*There were four big cylinders the size of paint cans beneath the hood. Output was 34 horsepower. Given the weight of the vehicle and its token bodywork, it was enough power to make the Mercer Raceabout a very fast car for its day.*

engine, a pair of goggles, and a lot of gumption. If conventional wisdom is correct and Henry Ford was responsible for putting America on wheels in the early 1900s, then Mercer was responsible for making those wheels go faster.

The Mercer Automobile Co. was established in 1910 in Mercer County, New Jersey. Its first cars were little more than two seats attached to a frame accented by a monocle windscreen, a large, round fuel tank mounted to the rear of the chassis, and scarcely enough coachwork to cover the large wooden artillery wheels and conceal the massive 300 cubic-inch, T-head four-cylinder engine. The company offered three models: the agile two-passenger Speedster (later renamed the Raceabout), a five-place Touring with more coachwork and seating, and a sporty Toy Tonneau four-passenger model. The Speedster, the most popular and most famous model, was equipped with a 3-speed selective transmission—later improved to a 4-speed in 1913—and a racy 34-horsepower output taken to the rear wheels by an oil-wetted multiple-disc clutch. In 1911, Mercer entered Speedsters in six races and came away with the winner's trophy five times. In 1912, the soon to be legendary Ralph DePalma set eight new records with a Speedster at the Los Angeles Speedway, and just to prove how race worthy a Mercer could be, Indy 500 driver Spencer Wishart drove one off the showroom floor of an Ohio dealer straight to a race in Columbus, where he won a 200-mile event, setting four new dirt track records in the process!

Mercer's successful run of racing victories between 1911 and 1916, with drivers like DePalma, Wishart, and Barney Oldfield, established the company as an early leader in motorsports. With Mercer, less was more, and despite its diaphanous bodywork, by 1913 the average price of a Raceabout was $2,500, a princely sum at that time.

As a company, Mercer was plagued by personal tragedy. Washington A. Robling II, the son of Mercer's founder, C. G. Robling, and the man responsible for the design of the Speedster, was lost when the Titanic sank in 1912. In 1917, F. W. Robling passed away, and a year later, so did C. G. Robling. The company managed to struggle along under different owners until around 1924, when the majority of assets were sold to the Philadelphia Mercer dealer Curran-McDevitt. A year later production in Mercer County, New Jersey, came to an end.

Enthusiasts consider the Mercer Raceabout among the greatest motorcars in American automotive history. It offers a driving experience that, even after 96 years, is still one of the most exciting in the world. ◆

*A windscreen was optional and omitted on this example. When one was ordered it was simply a beveled-edged monocle mounted on a brass stanchion. Brass was used for all of the brightwork including the radiator shell, headlamps, and trim. Chrome had not yet been invented.*

*Below. The firewall and dashboard were one and the same. Instruments were rudimentary and included water and oil temperature gauges. A Jones speedometer was mounted to the far left. The gear shift and handbrake were mounted on the right side of chassis.*

# *No.* 3

# 1932–1937 MODEL SJ DUESENBERG

## *America's Mightiest Motorcar*

**YOU PUT YOUR FOOT TO THE FLOOR;** the supercharger engages and the world sweeps by.

"Whenever I see a Duesenberg at a car show," says Jay Leno, "the first question I hear most people ask is, 'Hey, what's it worth?' That's a very hard question to answer. I once asked what it would cost to make some new Duesenberg cylinder heads to help keep the cars on the road and I was quoted a price of $210,000 each! A Duesenberg, nevertheless, is greater than the sum of its parts, or the cost of those parts. It is a monument to innovation, to perseverance, and relentless dedication to a single ideal . . . that in 1928 America could produce the finest automobile the world had ever known."

An automobile powered by a dual overhead cam, four-valve-per-cylinder engine sounds like a contemporary sports car, but that is exactly what Fred Duesenberg designed for the Model J straight eight engine back in 1928. When Fred added a supercharger of his own design in 1932, creating the 320-horsepower Model SJ, the Duesenberg became the most powerful road car ever built on either side of the Atlantic.

Even after three-quarters of a century, the bawl of eight supercharged cylinders at full song turns heads. When standing still the striking bodywork of an SJ roadster,

*The majority of Duesenberg owners were industrialists like the Vanderbilts, DuPonts, and Wrigleys. And there were film stars like Clark Gable and Gary Cooper, who both drove specially built 125-inch-wheelbase, supercharged speedsters. In the 1930s, the Model J became the celebrity car of the era, and movie studios had publicity photographs taken of their leading men seated behind the wheel or alongside a Duesenberg like this striking SJ roadster with handcrafted bodywork built in Pasadena, California, by the Walter M. Murphy Co. (Chip Connor collection)*

with its phalanx of chromed exhaust pipes pouring through the side of the hood, commands attention. Says Leno of the legendary SJ, "A great car, at least to my way of thinking, is any automobile that was better than it had to be, a car that was fast, agile, and capable of carrying its passengers in style. Those same qualities, which apply to a Duesenberg, equally suit a 1967 Lamborghini Miura, or a new Mercedes-Benz SLR McLaren. Our regard for these great motorcars has transcended the passing of time; it has become an emotional heirloom handed down from one generation to the next."

Supporting the engine, driveline, and bodywork was a Duesenberg-built chassis of unrivaled strength. Measuring either 142.5 or 153.5 inches in wheelbase, it was buttressed by six tubular cross members, anti-torque alloy-steel diagonal braces, and equipped with immense 15-inch x 3-inch hydraulic brakes, the largest in the industry. The rolling chassis alone won accolades for Fred Duesenberg. Then in 1932 he made it even better with the centrifugal supercharger. Delivering five psi of boost at 4,000 rpm, an SJ could accelerate from a standstill to 100 mph in just 17 seconds!

This was an unprecedented achievement in the automotive world of the 1930s. The SJ stood head and shoulders above any other car of the era by nearly

NOTHING QUITE SOUNDS LIKE A SUPERCHARGED DUESENBERG STRAIGHT EIGHT, AT FULL THROTTLE, WITH THE BLOWER ENGAGED, THE ENGINE HOWLS AND THE CAR GATHERS SPEED LIKE A RACEHORSE IN THE FINAL STRETCH. IT IS AS SOLID ON THE ROAD AS A LOCOMOTIVE, THIS IS DRIVING AT THE LIMIT FOR THE 1930S.

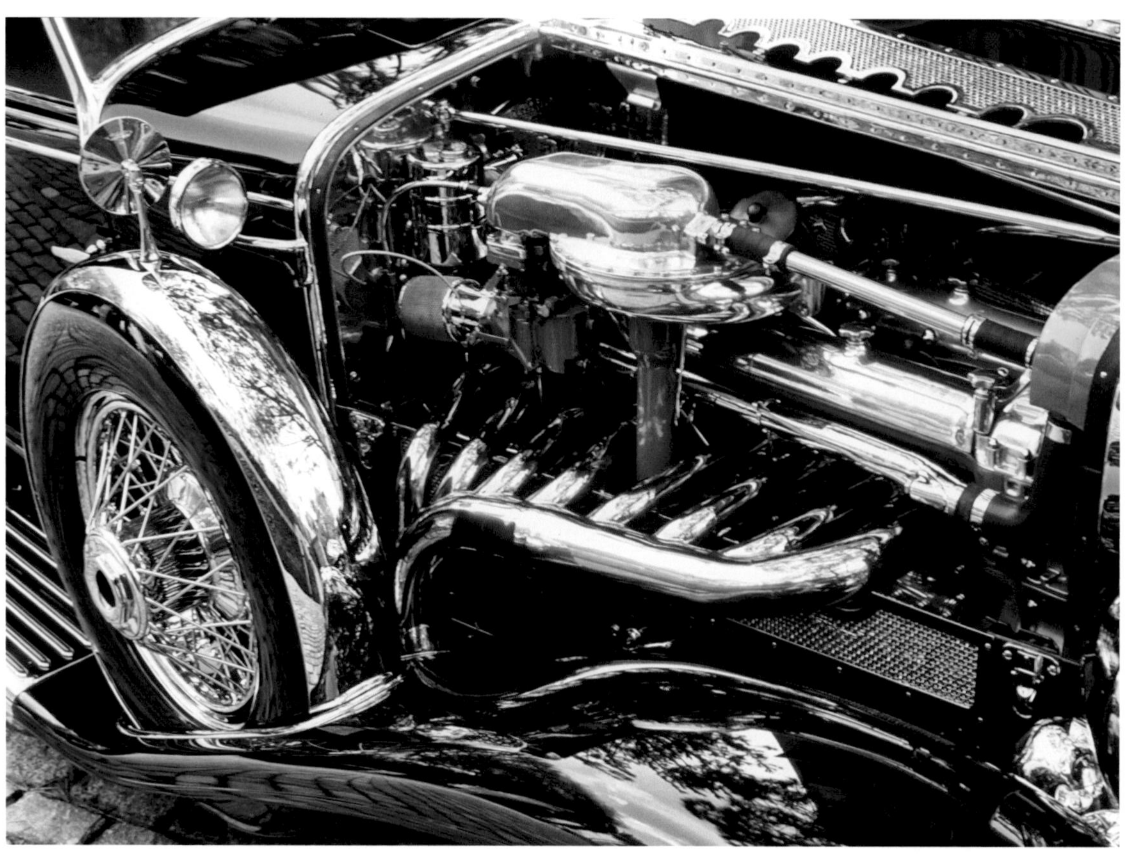

100 horsepower, regardless of engine displacement or number of cylinders. With a lightweight roadster body, an SJ could accelerate to 125 mph and cruise effortlessly up to 89 mph in second gear.

By the early 1930s, a Model J chassis sold for $8,500 and a supercharged SJ chassis cost $1,000 more. The average Duesenberg with the added cost of coachwork sold for $15,000 in the depths of the Great Depression. Because of the economic times and the cost of virtually hand-building these magnificent automobiles, no more than 485 were manufactured between 1928 and 1937, the year Duesenberg was forced to close its Indianapolis, Indiana, factory, bringing an end to one of the greatest American cars ever built. ◆

*Above. The greatest Duesenberg SJ ever was the Mormon Meteor, built in 1935 as a land speed record car for famed Salt Flats racer Ab Jenkins. On August 31, Jenkins would attain an average speed of 135.47 mph driving over a 10-mile oval laid out on the Utah Salt Flats. In 24 hours he traveled 3,262 miles—the same as driving from coast-to-coast in one day! At one point he maintained 152.124 mph for a full hour, and when he crossed the finish line after 24 hours, the Meteor was traveling at nearly 160 mph.*

*Opposite. The SJ carried its centrifugal supercharger mounted at the top of the engine, the most beautifully designed of the 1930s and perhaps of all time. Always trimmed in apple green, the SJ had chromed exhaust pipes that came through the hood and cascaded through the top of the fender. Most had four pipes surrounded by polished corrugated shrouds, while a handful, such as J498, were fitted with the rare Monel eight-port exhausts which glowed red hot when the car was driven hard.*

# 1955 Mercedes-Benz 300 SLR

## *Still One of the Hottest Rides of All Time*

**THERE ARE TWO SLR VERSIONS,** the competition roadsters, and two coupes built for Rudolf Uhlenhaut, Mercedes' chief engineer. After winning the 1952 racing season with the 300 SL, the factory set its sights on a new series of racecars for 1954. In the wake of the championship 300 SL came the 1954 W196 Formula One *monoposto* (with exposed front wheels) and its derivatives, the W196 streamliners and 300 SLR roadsters. The SLR sport versions arrived in the spring of 1955 with their engines enlarged in displacement to three liters.

### MAKING A CHAMPIONSHIP RACECAR

The change in displacement came as a result of the World Championship of Makes limit to three liters; thus for the SLRs the capacity of each cylinder was increased from 312 to 374 cubic centimeters, changing the overall swept volume from 2,496 to 2,992 cubic centimeters; just shy of three liters. Maximum engine speed was reduced to 7,600 rpm and the compression was 12.0:1. The SLR's power takeoff was from the center of the engine: a good news, bad news design. Power went through the front-mounted clutch to a rear-mounted 5-speed transmission. To keep the hood as low as possible, the engine was mounted at a 33-degree angle; however, as a result, the driveshaft now had to pass *under* the driver's seat! And this was the bad news. The driver had to operate the clutch pedal on the left and the accelerator and

*It may be the most exotic road car ever built, one of the two 300 SLR Gullwing Coupes designed and built for Mercedes' chief engineer Rudolf Uhlenhaut. In 1955 or 2008, this is still one of the hottest rides on the planet.*

brake on the right while straddling the driveshaft tunnel! Output from the 181.9 cubic inch straight eight was 310 horsepower at 7,500 rpm, with 230 lb-ft. of peak torque at 5,950 rpm. Depending upon the race, engine output varied from 276 brake horsepower at Le Mans, to 302 brake horsepower in the Swedish Grand Prix, and was reported to be as high as 345 brake horsepower, an almost unbelievable rating of nearly two horsepower per cubic inch.

IT ISN'T OFTEN THAT YOUR HEROES FROM THE PAST ARE STILL LIVING IN THE PRESENT. SHARE A MOMENT IN THE SAME SEAT OCCUPIED BY STIRLING MOSS IN 1955, AS HE STEERED ONE OF THE GREATEST RACE-CARS OF THE TWENTIETH CENTURY AROUND DUSTY ITALIAN ROADS. THE COCKPIT IS SMALL, THE DRIVE-SHAFT TUNNEL PASSES BETWEEN YOUR LEGS AND DISAPPEARS UNDER THE SEAT; THE FIRST THOUGHT THAT COMES TO MANY IS STRADDLING A SADDLE ON THE BACK OF A THOROUGHBRED RACEHORSE. EVERY-THING YOU NEED IS LAID OUT BEFORE YOU, THE REQUISITE GAUGES, THE WOOD-RIMMED STEERING WHEEL, AND THE GATED SHIFTER TO YOUR RIGHT.

By the time the SLRs were unveiled, Mercedes-Benz had introduced a production version of the 300 SL as a sports car, and owners, particularly in the U.S., were looking to Stuttgart for another season of racing victories to uphold the prominence of their shiny new German sports cars. For 1955 the premier venue would be Italy and the famed Mille Miglia.

*The cockpits were cramped and the driver had to straddle the drive-shaft tunnel with the clutch on the left, brake and throttle on the right. No left foot braking here!*

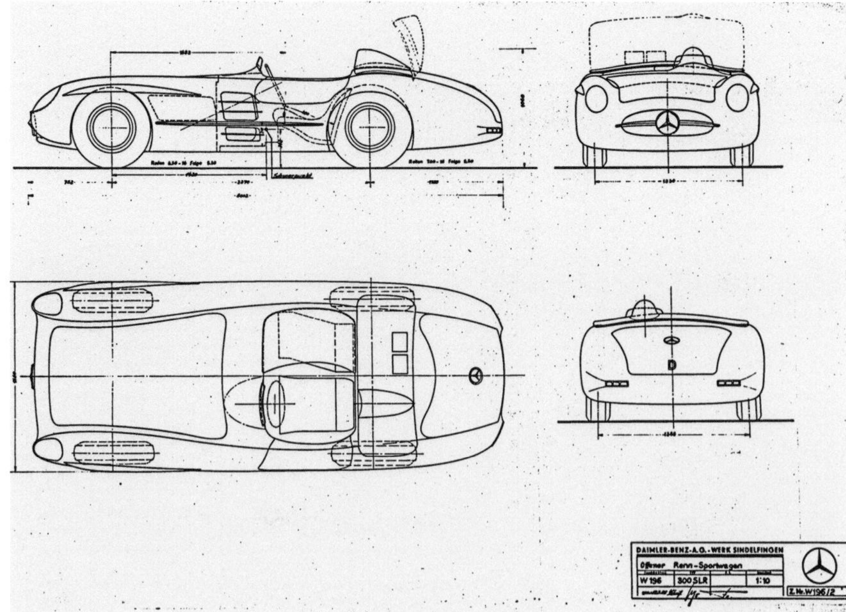

*The blueprint for the 300 SLR shows the design of the airbrake.*

In May 1955, the race followed a route over public roads through the center of Italy, from Brescia in the north to Rome in the south and back along a different route.

"My friend Denis Jenkinson, a brilliant automotive journalist and motorcycle racer, was teamed with me," says Sir Stirling as clearly as through it were yesterday. "After methodically pre-running the course, Jenks and I had it down to the extent that I would later rely on him to tell me by hand signals how to approach every turn, which he had mapped out, condensing the critical points of that 1,000-mile course into a handwritten paper roller of route notes 15 feet, 6 inches long. On May 2, we won the Mille Miglia in the record time of 10 hours, 7 minutes, and 48 seconds with the 300 SLR." That record has never been broken. Behind Moss, Mercedes team cars finished in 2nd and 4th, just a few minutes off of a 1-2-3 sweep. Wrote Jenkinson: "It would have been difficult to find a more successful sports/racing car and certainly one so advanced technically."

## THE BODY BEAUTIFUL

The 300 SLR's body was made from a tough yet malleable form of sheet magnesium. Capable of speeds in excess of 185 mph, the cars used massive inboard brakes and an innovative hydraulic airbrake to scrub off speed. The airbrake was one of the SLR's most remarkable features.

"The idea for this wind brake," explains Sir Stirling, "came from director of motorsports Alfred Neubauer, who was looking to develop a system to reduce the wear on conventional brakes and tires during long-distance races such as Le Mans and Rheims. Neubauer wanted to use wind resistance to slow the car. When deployed, the downward load imposed was arranged to pass through the center of gravity of the car. And as well as providing additional braking, it also increased the adhesion of the tires due to the downward pressure." Two hydraulic arms raised the entire rear decklid, and a lever operated by the driver opened a valve elevating the flap. Moss, who had one of the best seasons ever behind the wheel of an SLR, said of the airbrake, "It feels as if a giant hand had reached down and grabbed the car by the rear end." Originally a linkage was fitted to the gear lever mechanism so that when the driver selected second gear the airbrake automatically lowered. However, Moss discovered he could use the airbrake for most corners and further reduce wear on the wheel brakes. He could also corner better at some points by putting the airbrake only halfway up, thus increasing the load on the tires! As a result, the SLRs were quickly modified so that the airbrake could be operated completely by the driver.

## COUPES TO STIR THE SOUL AND UNNERVE THE COMPETITION

The two SLR Gullwing Coupes built for Uhlenhaut were essentially road-going racecars. They first appeared on the road in 1955. Looking like a 300 SL Gullwing that had attended NFL training camp, its long hood was complemented by side-mounted exhaust pipes, dramatic air vents, and a cockpit with wraparound windshield. Uhlenhaut referred to his latest automotive work of art as a "hot-heeled touring car." He would systematically arrive at a race ahead of the team and scream into the pits. This brought no small amount of attention from other teams, who immediately wondered, "What are their racecars like?" when they saw Mercedes' chief engineer alight from within.

Uhlenhaut's new coupe recorded a speed of 180 mph during a test conducted by *Automobil Revue* magazine at 4 A.M. on a closed section of motorway outside Munich. "We are driving a car which barely takes a second to overtake the rest of the traffic and for which 120 mph on a quiet motorway is little more than walking pace. With its unflappable handling through corners, it treats the laws of centrifugal force with apparent disdain," scribbled the lucky test reporter after a total of more than 2,000 miles. His only regret was that this was a sports car "which we will never be able to buy and which the average driver would never buy anyway." Half a century later that sentiment has changed. The new Mercedes-Benz SLR McLaren is very much a modern realization of the legendary Uhlenhaut Coupes. ◆

*There were two versions of the 300 SLR, the roadsters used for racing in 1955 (pictured with Moss driving) and two Gullwing Coupes built for chief engineer Rudolf Uhlenhaut. (Photo courtesy MBNA)*

# No. 5

## 1961 Maserati Tipo 63/64

### *It's Only a Racecar in a Gilded Cage*

**IT'S HARD TO MAKE A LIST** of great automobiles to drive without picking a few vintage racecars, and few are as alluring as the swoopy Italian masterpiece known admiringly by sports car aficionados simply as, the "Birdcage."

When it comes to body styling, the Birdcage Maserati is as crisp and cool as the other side of your pillow.

APPREHENSION IS YOUR FIRST EMOTION WHEN YOU IGNITE THE ENGINE. THIS IS AN UNTAMED BEAST THAT DEMANDS EVERYTHING AND ONLY GIVES BACK WHAT IT GETS. THE BODY SITS VERY LOW TO THE GROUND; EVERY BUMP IN THE ROAD CAN BE FELT THROUGH THE SUSPENSION AND STEERING. IT IS UNFORGIVING HERE. THE MASERATI MUST BE DRIVEN HARD, BUT WITH DEFT HANDS ON THE WHEEL AND SHIFTER.

Sitting at almost ground level in the cockpit, surrounded by the open framework of the Maserati's chassis, one can easily envision the sensations of other racecars screaming alongside, dropping back or darting ahead as you come into a turn. This becomes the most visceral of all the cars we have chosen. Your feet search out

*Originally fitted with a Tipo 63 body, chassis 63002 was returned to the factory and updated with the more stylish Tipo 64 body, regarded by nearly all enthusiasts as the most beautiful of the Birdcage Maseratis.*

*The high crowned fenders and wide stance of the Tipo 64 body give the car its low slung appearance. The narrow windscreen also contributes to the look.*

three drilled alloy pedals tucked somewhere near the firewall. Straight ahead a simple, slim-rimmed three-spoke steering wheel falls directly at hand. Behind it, an engine-turned metal dashboard with just the necessities: a Jaeger tachometer, oil and water temperature gauges, oil pressure gauge, ammeter, and nothing more. On the floor to your right, a short gear selector rises up to your hand. It's time to go racing.

Light up the V12 Maserati engine buried somewhere behind in a maze of framework and there ensures a cacophony that both deafens and rewards the senses. From the moment you let off the clutch you feel the heart of this brute. Crude, perhaps, because it rattles and shakes and carries on like a racehorse refusing to enter the gate. But once you let it go, once the raspy exhaust note fills the air, it is perfection, albeit unrefined. The Maserati leaves you hungry for a long straight road, long enough to reach fifth gear and 8,500 rpm.

The Birdcage body is a lightweight amalgam of panels attached by Dzus fasteners to a labyrinth of tiny welded tubes. It is as close to a technically perfect space frame as possible for the 1960s. The Birdcage is, after all, an artifact, part of an illustrious history that began 81 years ago with Alfieri Maserati's victory in the 1926 Targa Florio and the establishment of Officini Alfieri Maserati, with the head of Neptune's Trident as the company's trademark.

There were several variations of the Birdcage design from the late 1950s through the early 1960s with changes in engine type and placement, four and twelve cylinders, front and mid-mounted, and different body designs, from somewhere north of ugly in 1957–59 with the Tipo 60/61 to the breathtaking Tipo

63/64, the 64 being the body style pictured. The 63 had somewhat of a pinched nose and a higher windscreen, whereas the wider visage of the Tipo 64 becomes the quintessential Maserati of the 1960s when it comes to looks. Ironically, the 60/61 were more successful in racing.

The car pictured has an interesting history. Starting life as a Tipo 63, it was returned to the factory by American sportsman Briggs Cunningham and refitted with the Tipo 64 body. Cunningham later replaced the Maserati V12 with a Tipo 61 four-cylinder engine, claiming that the high-strung fours were more competitive. ◆

*Right. The driver is wedged into the seat surrounded by the structural tubing of the birdcage. The pedals can just barely be seen ahead of the cowl.*

*Below. The mid-engine design of the Tipo 63/64—the original "cab forward" look—placed the driver at the extreme front of the body with the pedals virtually in the nose of the car.*

# 1955 Porsche 550 Spyder

## A Tragic Road to Fame

"DREAM AS IF YOU'LL LIVE FOREVER. LIVE AS IF YOU'LL DIE TODAY."
— JAMES DEAN

**OPENING SCENE:** An old black Bakelite business telephone sitting on a highly polished mahogany desk. Just out of focus in the background, the viewer sees the shapes of small sports cars on a showroom floor. The phone rings and the distant shape of a man turns and walks toward it. Coming into focus, he picks up the receiver and answers.

"Hoffman Motors."

There is a moment's hesitation and his expression suddenly turns distraught.

"Just a minute, I'll get Mr. Hoffman."

The salesman walks quickly across the showroom floor and interrupts an impeccably dressed, balding gentleman standing with two customers. He whispers into his ear.

"There is a reporter from the *New York Times* on the telephone. He wants information about the Porsche 550 Spyder." The salesman pauses as if to gather his nerve before continuing. "James Dean was killed in one yesterday afternoon."

The camera pulls back to reveal Hoffman's Manhattan showroom with 356 coupes, cabriolets, and a 550 Spyder on display.

*Seen from above, the beautiful styling of the 550 Spyder becomes evident, as does its simplicity. The engine cover, for example, was simply held to the rear cowl by a pair of leather straps. The interior was little more than two bucket seats, steering wheel, pedals, gearbox, and necessary gauges. (Photo by Dennis Adler from the Peter Halper collection)*

*The Type 547 four-cam engine, positioned forward of the rear axle, took up only a small portion of the space behind the cowl. The spare tire consumed the rest. The fuel tank was under the front decklid. (Porsche A.G. and author's archives)*

Close-up of Hoffman and the salesman: Hoffman leans in.

"The one from von Neumann?" he asks rhetorically, bringing his fingertips to his mouth. "Tragic." He taps his index finger to his lips. "Very tragic." Hoffman excuses himself from the two gentlemen, introduces his associate, and turns toward the sales desk. Fade to black.

## IMMORTALITY AND DEATH

It was on September 30, 1955, that one of America's most charismatic and promising young actors drove into cinematic and automotive immortality behind the wheel of a new Porsche 550 Spyder. That tragic event would forever link Dean's name to Porsche and make more Americans aware of the small, imported German sports cars than all the advertising in the world. It is ironic how one detail can change an event; a traffic accident that normally would have attracted little more than mention in the pages of a local Northern California newspaper suddenly became an international headline because the driver was James Dean.

The allure of the 550 Spyder that attracted James Dean has never diminished. Even today there are few sports cars more exciting to drive. Not that Porsche 550s are that fast or agile by modern standards, but because like so many historic automobiles they were, at one point in time, the state of the art, and to drive them today is to know what it was like to live at that moment in time.

## THE RACECAR AND THE ROAD CAR

The body design was a work of purposeful art penned by Erwin Komenda, father of the legendary Porsche 356. The sweep of the fender line was far more graceful than the original racecars campaigned by the factory in 1953, the contours more visually appealing and

(Photo illustration created By Dennis Adler for the "James Dean Story" published in Car Collector Magazine, September 2005)

*James Dean was the most charismatic actor of his generation. Reflecting on Dean's life, in 1993, newspaper columnist George Will wrote, ". . . Dean played himself—a mumbling, arrested-development adolescent—to perfection." James Dean perhaps saw himself in another light, as a man who loved two things in his life, being someone else in front of a camera, and himself behind the wheel of a racecar.*

*Driver Johnny Claes at Le Mans in 1954 heads toward a class finish (1.5-liter) and 12th overall in the 24 Hours. Remarkably, the car, co-driven by Paul Stasse, finished on only three cylinders! (Porsche A.G. photo)*

accented by raised rear fenders. The aluminum bodies were produced by Karosserie Wendler in Reutlingen and weighed a mere 200 pounds. A tubular ladder frame based on the racecar design carried the lightweight bodywork and Porsche's latest version of the 547 four-cam engine. Although introduced at the Paris Salon as a finished car in 1953, the final version of the 550 Spyder would require another year of revisions before going into limited production.

Porsche had designated the production models as the 550/1500RS, which stood for the type, 550; the approximate engine displacement, 1,500 cubic centimeters; and designation, *Rennsport*, or sports racing. The Spyder epithet was New York importer Max Hoffman's idea, believing that a name, rather than a series of numbers, would be more marketable to Americans. Among sports car cognoscenti, the Spyder (or Spider) classification was already familiar, having been used to describe very light, sketchy two-seater competition sports cars since the 1930s.

At the heart of the 550/1500RS was the latest version of the Type 547 four-cam engine developing 110 horsepower. With its lightweight body and frame, the dry weight ranged between 1,320 and 1,350 pounds, depending on the equipment fitted. As for price, the cars boasted a delivery nearly twice that of a standard Porsche 356, exceeding $6,800 in the United States. To put that in perspective, a brand new Cadillac Eldorado sold for $5,738 in 1954.

The 550 Spyders came with either a racing screen for the driver, with a passenger-side tonneau cover, or a full-width low racing screen. The car could also be ordered with a conventional aluminum-framed safety glass windscreen and a simple canvas top, a combination seldom seen these days as most were intended for racing.

## JAMES DEAN AND THE 550

Of all the people who owned 550s, Dean was the most famous. He had just finished filming *Giant* and was anxious to get back into a racecar. He purchased the 550 from John von Neumann in September 1955, a few weeks before his fatal crash. The accident occurred on a remote California highway just outside Cholame, his 550 struck nearly head on by a 1950 Ford coupe that crossed the centerline and turned into his path. The Porsche looked liked a crumpled pack of cigarettes, its aluminum body twisted, its famous-faced driver dead. Dean's passenger, Porsche mechanic Rolf Wütherich, was thrown clear and miraculously survived the accident with only minor injuries.

IT IS MISLEADING. THE LOOK IS SLEEK, THE SOUND OF THE ENGINE BRASH, IT IS SMALL AND ALMOST UNASSUMING BUT WHEN THE GEARS ARE ENGAGED AND THE ROAD UNWINDS IN FRONT OF YOU, A PORSCHE 550 IS INTOXICATING. DESPITE ITS POWER, THE FLAT-OPPOSED ENGINE SOUNDS LIKE A CAN OF NICKELS BEING SHAKEN, THE SHIFTER IS WOBBLY AND EVERYTHING ABOUT THE INTERIOR IS MINIMALIST. DRIVE IT HARD ON THE STRAIGHTAWAYS, DECLINING RADIUS TURNS, AND SWITCHBACKS OF A ROAD COURSE, DO IT RIGHT, RESPECT THE CAR'S TEMPERAMENT, AND THE 550 WILL TAKE YOUR BREATH AWAY SWEEPING AROUND A RACETRACK LIKE IT IS ON RAILS. BUT NEVER FORGET, THE 550 IS UNFORGIVING.

## A TRAGIC STORY

While filming *Giant,* Dean made a 30-second promotional commercial for the National Highway Safety Committee. In it Dean said, "I used to fly around quite a bit, took a lot of unnecessary chances on the highway. Now when I drive on the highway, I'm extra cautious." He added that he leaves the fast driving for the racetrack. Before the scene ended, Dean told the audience to "Take it easy driving. The life you save might be mine." ◆

14

# 1961 Ferrari 250 GT (SWB) Short Wheelbase Berlinetta

## *The Hottest Sports Car of the Early Sixties*

**WHILE MOST SPORTS CAR** enthusiasts rave about the 250 GTO, that legendary Ferrari actually evolved from the 250 GT SWB, the Short Wheelbase Berlinetta. In 1962, Enzo Ferrari told the Fédération Internationale de l'Automobile, when they questioned him regarding the company's failure to build enough 250 GTOs to meet homologation, "The market for such a car was already saturated and there were only a few men in the world who could master its ferocity!" Given that the 250 GTO, the Gran Turismo Omologato, was regarded by Ferrari as an "improved version" of the 250 GT SWB, the F.I.A., after counting all the SWBs that had been built, acquiesced to Ferrari's position and homologated the 250 GTO without further question. Only Enzo Ferrari could have stood up to the F.I.A. and won. His argument, however, was valid. The 250 GT SWB was the basis for the GTO.

The SWB arrived on the heels of another great Berlinetta, the 250 GT Tour de France. As Sergio Pininfarina explained to the author some years ago, a Berlinetta by definition is ". . . a lightweight, streamlined body trimmed for racing—this being the distinguishing characteristic between a Berlinetta and a traditional coupe." Berlinetta literally means "little sedan" in Italian.

*Giotto Bizzarrini, Carlo Chiti, and Mauro Forghieri developed the 250 GT (SWB) Short Wheelbase Berlinetta in 1959. The car's wheelbase measured only 94.5 inches. The example shown, serial number 2689, is owned today by Bruce Meyer. In 1961 this car won the GT class at Le Mans. It is one of only five ultra lightweight factory cars built specifically for the 1961 race.*

*Above. Every Ferrari dashboard was designed to be functional but not always attractive. As a purebred racecar the SWB's interior fell into the latter category.*

*Opposite. On the short 94.5-inch wheelbase, the blunt looking fastback was only 163.5 inches (13.6 feet) long. With the fuel filler coming through the left rear fender, a splash shield was mounted above the left exhaust pipes, just in case of a fuel spill.*

## A PURPOSE-BUILT INTERIOR

SWB interiors were generally afforded minimal trim, insulation, and accessories, making them louder and less comfortable but not unbearable. As each car was essentially built to order, some were more luxuriously appointed than others. The SWB was by no means a typical Ferrari road car.

The principal designer was Giotto Bizzarrini, who would later go on to build his own cars. With a wheelbase measuring only 94.5 inches, the SWB utilized an otherwise outdated solid rear axle but located in such a way that a more modern independent rear suspension would have provided no advantage. The front suspension used wishbones and coil springs with an antiroll bar, the rigid axle rear, leaf springs, and radius arms.

Bizzarrini's goal had been to improve the handling of the longer wheelbase 250 GT, and this he skillfully accomplished with the SWB. Although the pure road car, or Lusso, models were more softly sprung, the hard suspension of the competition version gave the SWB terrific cornering power in exchange for its harsher ride.

## A WINNING REPUTATION BEFORE THE FIRST WIN

The 250 GT SWB was one of those rare cars that, from the moment it was introduced, became highly desirable, especially among privateer (independent) race drivers. With its short 94.5-inch wheelbase, overall length was a mere 163.5 inches, (13.6 feet). The blunt-looking fastback carried the classic Colombo-designed sixty-degree, 3-liter V12 beneath its elongated hood. As a result of the shorter overall length, reduced weight, and increased output—280 horsepower at 7,000 rpm versus 260 horsepower at 7,000 rpm for the Tour de France—the SWB was faster and handled better than its predecessor, making it an even more ominous competitor. All of the cars were equipped with 4-speed synchromesh gearboxes, and later models were offered with electric overdrive. The 250 GT SWB Berlinetta was also the first GT Ferrari offered with disc brakes, and it was the hit of the Paris Motor Show in October 1959. Order books were soon full, much to the frustration of would-be owners who were given no delivery date if their names were not known to be directly related to racing!

**THE SWB UNLEASHES THE MOST HORSEPOWER OF ANY CAR YOU CAN DRIVE FROM THIS PERIOD AND THE EXPERIENCE IS FELT THROUGH EVERY BONE IN YOUR BODY AS THE STIFF COMPETITION SUSPENSION HOLDS THE CAR FIRM TO THE PAVEMENT, THE TIRES SQUEAL, AND THE CONCERT OF THE TRANSMISSION AND EXHAUST FILL YOUR HEAD WITH MECHANICAL EMOTIONS THAT MATCH YOUR EVERY SHIFT AND TURN OF THE WHEEL.**

Not only was the SWB a stunning performer, it

was a strikingly handsome car. In creating a body to fit the shortened wheelbase, designer Sergio Pininfarina eliminated the use of quarter windows, creating an aggressive profile that situated the power of the body over the wheels, like a crouching cat. Most of the bodies were steel, with aluminum doors, hoods, and trunk lids, although a few were constructed entirely of alloy for competition. The doors, hoods, and decklids were all constructed in Modena at the *atelier* of Sergio Scaglietti.

As a road car it was without peer, and in competition the SWBs began a cannonade across Europe in 1960. The new Ferraris won the Tourist Trophy race in England, the Tour de France, and the 1000km of Paris at Montlhéry. In 1961, Stirling Moss won the Tourist Trophy for Ferrari a second time. During 1961, so many class wins were collected by Short Wheelbase Berlinettas that by season's end Ferrari owned the GT class in the Constructors' Championship.

With a top speed of around 150 mph, it was one of the fastest sports cars of its time and a driver's car with nimble handling and superb balance that allowed it to be driven hard into corners as well as flat out on a straightaway. There were fewer than 200 examples built from late 1959 until early 1963 in both competition and road car versions. The car pictured is one of the most famous of all the 250 SWB models. Chassis 2689, this factory racecar, fitted with an all-alloy body (one of five built for the race at Le Mans), was first in class in 1961, first overall at Monza in 1961, first in class at the 1961 1000km at

*Le Mans 1961. The 250 GT SWB races on to win its class in the 24-hour day-into-night marathon. (Photo from Bruce Meyer collection)*

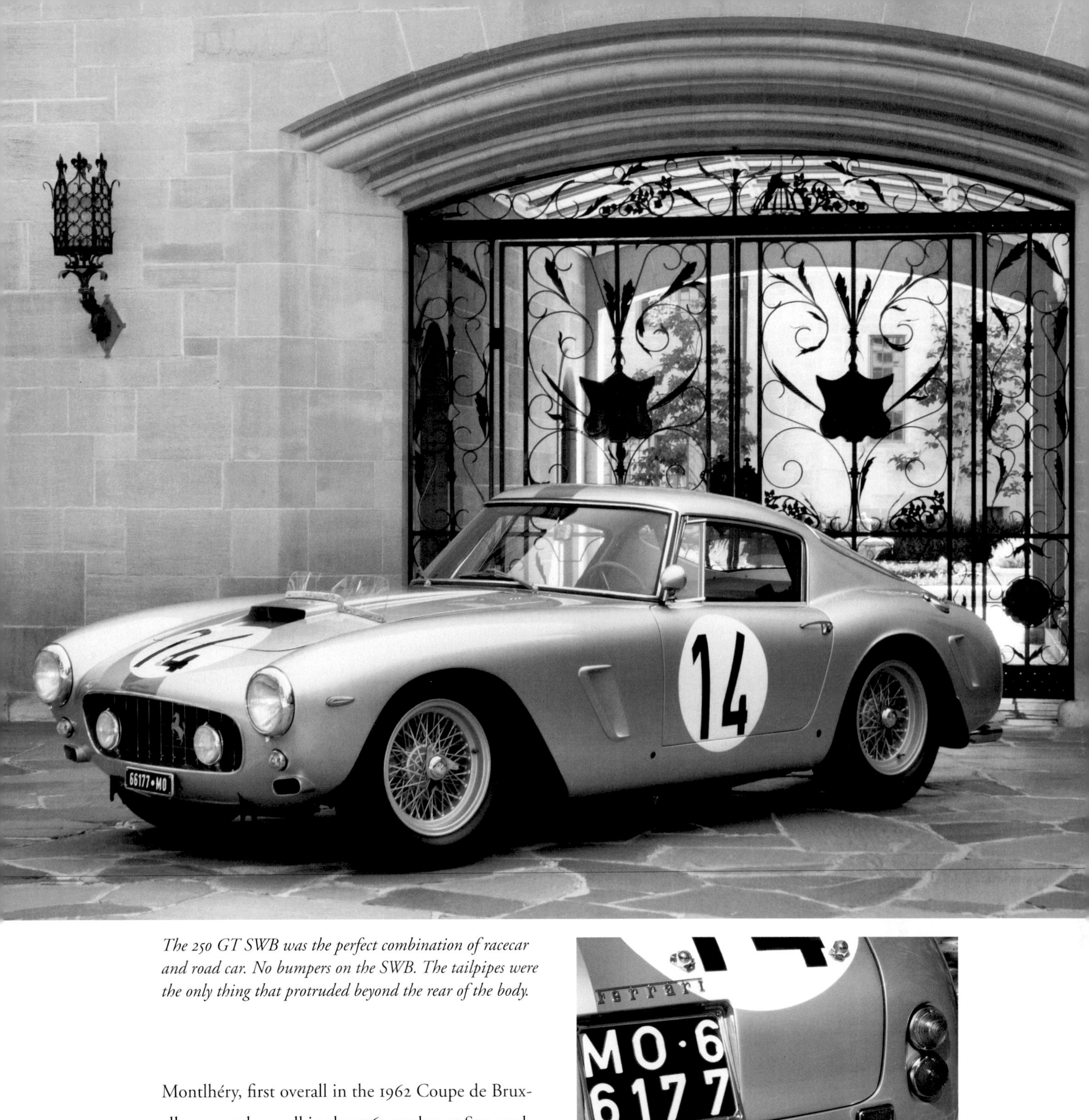

*The 250 GT SWB was the perfect combination of racecar and road car. No bumpers on the SWB. The tailpipes were the only thing that protruded beyond the rear of the body.*

Montlhéry, first overall in the 1962 Coupe de Bruxelles, second overall in the 1962 500km at Spa, and second in class at the 1962 Nürburgring 1000km. These special competition cars were further equipped with higher-output engines delivering 285 horsepower. One achieved a top speed of 160 mph recorded down the Mulsanne Straight at Le Mans. A heroic car for heroic drivers, it's a mechanical masterpiece that begs to be driven. ◆

JAGUAR

# 1955 Jaguar D-Type

## A Different Breed of Cat

**JAGUAR'S POST WORLD WAR II** resurrection in 1946 led to the creation of one of the most important sports cars of the 1950s, the Jaguar XK-120. While the car was a landmark design, it was not a purebred racecar, though these early Jaguars acquitted themselves nicely in sports car racing. It was competition XK-120 C and D Types, however, which brought the laurels to Coventry's doorstep.

In Europe, both factory backed and independently raced XK-120 Jags cut a wide swath through the competition, even at Le Mans, where, although severely

> STUFFED INTO THE COCKPIT WITH A SHALLOW WINDSCREEN AND A MILE-LONG HOOD AHEAD, THE SOUND OF THE ENGINE AND EXHAUST FILL YOUR HEAD AND THE ONLY THING THAT MATTERS IS THE NEXT CURVE IN THE ROAD.

outclassed, they still finished a respectable 12th and 15th. The lessons learned in 1950 brought forth an entirely new effort from Coventry in 1951, and Jaguar returned to Le Mans with the remarkable XK-120 C-Types.

Raymond "Lofty" England, who managed the Jaguar Racing Team from 1951 to 1956, said that the XK-120 C-Types were designed to increase the potential of otherwise standard mechanicals. Indeed, the racecars used stock engines, gearboxes, and axle units but these were surrounded by lighter, more aerodynamically shaped

*The twenty-eighth car built in the D-Type series was an export to the United States in 1955 and appeared in the May 1956 issue of* Road & Track. *In America, D-Types quickly found their way in SCCA events at Watkins Glen, the Palm Springs Airport races, Santa Barbara, Riverside, Pomona, and Pebble Beach. The cost of the car in 1955 was $9,875.*

*Delivering a conservatively estimated 250 horsepower at 6,000 rpm and 242 lb-ft. of torque at 4,000 rpm, the D-Type's production-based dual overhead cam six-cylinder engine was fed the air/fuel mix through three 45mm-diameter dual Weber carburetors. Zero-to-60 times averaged 4.7 seconds.*

bodies. With that combination, England believed Jaguar had a chance of winning Le Mans and in 1951 his team did just that, with a stunning 1-2-3 finish. And Le Mans was not the only success that year; the Jaguars were also victorious in the Belgian Marathon de la Route, Alpine, Tulip, and RAC Rallies, while Stirling Moss repeated his win in the Tourist Trophy. In America, Jaguars scored wins at Watkins Glen, New York, at Reno, Nevada, and in virtually every Jaguar dealership across the nation.

The following year, England and the Jaguar team faced Mercedes-Benz and watched as their Le Mans title was wrested away from them by the most advanced sports cars in the world—the 300 SL, a racecar that had been completely inspired by Jag's 1951 Jaguar XK-120 C.

With Mercedes-Benz skipping the 1953 and 1954 seasons, Jaguar faced a new challenger at Le Mans in 1953, Ferrari and world champion driver Alberto Ascari. In the end, Jaguar prevailed, with the Tony Rolt/Duncan Hamilton C-Type finishing 1$^{st}$, the Stirling Moss/Peter Walker car in 2$^{nd}$, and the Peter Whitehead/Ian Stewart C-Type in 4$^{th}$. Jaguar had been very fortunate. Ferrari had been challenged and beaten. This would not be forgotten.

For 1954 Jaguar was back with a new racecar, the D-Type, fitted with an even more streamlined aluminum body created by company founder William Lyons and his aerodynamics specialist, Malcolm Sayer. Six inches lower than the C-Type, with a 90.6-inch wheelbase and 154-inch overall length, the cars were equipped with improved disc brakes, light-alloy wheels, dry-sump lubrication, and even more horsepower.

Unfortunately, it was not to be Jaguar's year. At Le Mans, bad weather plagued the cars throughout.

Moss lost his brakes at the end of the long *Mulsanne* and retired on the spot. He had, however, set a record top speed for the Mulsanne Straight of 172.97 mph. A second car suffered gearbox failure, while the third, driven by 1953 winners Hamilton and Rolt, fought unsuccessfully throughout the race to overtake the leader. This year Jaguar would have to settle for a 2nd place behind Ferrari.

Mercedes-Benz and Jaguar would face off once again at Le Mans in 1955. Both were counting on their latest cars and top drivers. The improved D-Type Jaguar pictured and the new 300 SLR Mercedes were equally matched. Mercedes pinned its hopes on Juan Manuel Fangio, while Jaguar had Mike Hawthorn. The ill-fated race would end in tragedy and the withdrawal of Mercedes-Benz from the race, giving Hawthorn and Jaguar the victory.

For the next two seasons, the D-Types were virtually unbeatable, with every victory enhancing the company's reputation. Even after Jaguar withdrew from racing in 1956, a private team won Le Mans in 1957. In fact, Jaguar won the great event five times in seven years, with a combination of C-Type and D-Type sports cars.

Driving a D-Type today is an experience few people can share. The D-Type Jaguars remain one of the most significant sports racing cars of the twentieth century. ◆

*Short on space and amenities, the D-Type was equipped with only essential gauges; this view over the cockpit (with the co-driver tonneau removed) reveals the 4-speed shift lever and hand brake, tachometer (redlined at 6,500 rpm), and a glimpse of the speedometer.*

BUGATTI

# 1939 Type 57C Bugatti

## *Swift Elegance in the French Idiom*

**THERE WAS A TIME WHEN ART** and fashion shared a place with automotive design, and whether it was the stroke of an artist's brush, the cut of an elegant gown, or the flowing coachwork of a luxurious car one sought, the foremost place in the world to find it was Paris.

In France, the design and construction of custom coachwork had developed into an art form known as *Goutte d'eau*, which literally translated is a drop of water. For automobiles the meaning was less literal, and coachwork of this type was referred to as "teardrop" styling. The masters of *Goutte d'eau* were Joseph Figoni and Jacques Saoutchik.

Throughout the 1930s, French coachbuilders had been fascinated with aerodynamics and were continually searching for ways to cheat the wind. Most of the coachwork by Saoutchik and Figoni was on the National marques and particularly Bugatti, the most celebrated automaker in France.

The Bugatti factory was located at Molsheim in Alsace, an occasionally disputed borderline between France and Germany. Ettore Bugatti, "Le Patron" or "The Boss" as many of his associates, and his sons, called him, was to this small region of France what Henry Ford was to Dearborn, Michigan. From around 1910 to 1951, nearly 8,000 cars bearing the Bugatti signature were produced.

The factory was run by Ettore and later by his son Jean, a brilliant automotive designer and stylist. From the time he was 20, Jean's domain was the styling studio,

*Although Jean Bugatti created a number of splendid body styles for the Type 57, France's leading coachbuilders produced many stunning one-of-a-kind bodies to fit the Type 57 chassis, such as this majestic roadster designed by Jacques Saoutchik in 1939.*

*Known for exotic styling, Saoutchik's most avant-garde design was this Type 57C. The rear contours are nearly identical to bodies designed by Joseph Figoni during the same era. Chrome was used to accent the body lines, particularly the rear decklid, one of the car's most impressive attributes.*

and his designs, though often controversial, were among the most stirring of the era. What he created in the brief period from 1931, when he took over management of the factory, until 1939, when he died tragically in a traffic accident, have become the most celebrated of Bugatti sports and touring cars.

During his tenure as acting director, Jean designed the greatest motorcar ever to bear the company's famed horseshoe grille: the Type 57. From the time of its introduction in 1934 to the assembly of the last models less than a year after the start of World War II, a total of 670 Type 57, 57S, 57C, and 57SC model were manufactured, more than any Bugatti. A Bugatti was a rare car even when new.

## MODERNIZING AN OLD IDEA

The Type 57 was the first Bugatti to integrate the gearbox with the engine, using a single dry-plate clutch in the housing between, and a new 4-speed transmission operated through helical constant mesh

THE BEST DESCRIPTION OF GETTING BEHIND THE WHEEL OF A BUGATTI TYPE 57 IS THAT OF TRYING ON A SUIT THAT FITS IN ALL THE RIGHT PLACES AND MAKES YOU FEEL LIKE A MILLION DOLLARS. ONE DOES NOT SO MUCH RIDE IN A TYPE 57 AS BECOME A PART OF IT. THE DRIVER IS AT THE HEART OF A MACHINE DESIGNED TO DO WHAT ETTORE BUGATTI DEEMED MOST IMPORTANT: GO FAST, CORNER SMOOTHLY, AND THEN GO FASTER.

gears on second, third, and top. The cars could also be ordered with the marvelous Cotal electro-mechanical pre-selector gearbox favored by race drivers.

The original 3.3-liter straight eight used in the Type 57 was based on Jean's earlier Type 50 design, utilizing a six-main bearing crankshaft, integral head and block, and two valves per cylinder actuated by Miller-inspired dual overhead camshafts. Displacing 3,257 cubic centimeters, output from the early engines was 135 horsepower.

The engine was as much a work of art as the hand-built coachwork that surrounded it. The labor that went into its construction, and that of the engine compartment itself, is almost unparalleled—engine covers hand scribed in a vaguely geometric pattern, and a meticulously damascened and polished firewall, traits which have come to represent the Bugatti style.

*Bugatti interiors were simple in design. The Saoutchik car is upholstered in red leather, a brilliant but not overstated contrast to the black body. One of the most unusual features on the Saoutchik Bugatti is the clock mounted in the hub of the steering wheel.*

The suspension was based on the traditional Bugatti design pioneered by Ettore, a solid rear axle using quarter-elliptic springs, and in front, one of the most complex and exotic designs ever conceived, Bugatti's unique solid beam open-boxed axle with semi-elliptic front springs passing through the axle shaft. This has always been an object of fascination.

On the inside, and in considerable contrast to the exterior styling, Bugatti kept his instruments and controls relatively simple, disinclined as he was to overstate the fundamentals of operation. Wood was the usual medium for the dashboard. Gauges were large and few, placed within clear view of the driver.

There were three additional versions of the Type 57, the 57S (S for Sport), introduced in 1935 with a more powerful, higher compression engine, and shorter 117.5-inch wheelbase, (versus the original 130-inch). At the end of 1936, Bugatti switched to the improved Series 2 chassis in preparation for the new 200-horsepower supercharged Type 57C, and finally, the 57SC, which sported a shorter wheelbase and was intended principally for racing.

A year before Jean's fatal accident, he introduced the Series 3 chassis, featuring Bugatti-Lockheed designed hydraulic brakes and a twin master cylinder.

*There were four Type 57 engines produced, this being the third, the Type 57C supercharged variant introduced at the end of 1936 on the Series 2 chassis. The 57C developed 200 horsepower, making it one of the fastest cars in the world in 1936.*

The majority of the bodies for Type 57 chassis were designed by Jean; however, chassis were also bodied by several of France's leading *carrosserie*, including the renowned house of Saoutchik.

The stunning coachwork on this black 1939 Roadster is believed to be the only two-passenger Type 57C designed by the renowned French stylist. The use of chrome embellishment over the entire length of the car is representative of Saoutchik and Figoni designs, but Saoutchik was a bit more flamboyant with the use of chromed flashing for the rear decklid fin, bumper, and teardrop fender tips. The car is almost more striking from the rear than head on, where the bold, Bugatti horseshoe grille is balanced by pontoon-style fenders and chrome-trimmed headlights. This body on any car would have been spectacular; on a Bugatti Type 57C it was simply breathtaking. ◆

*Bugatti's famous horseshoe grille was symbolic, as the Bugatti family also owned and bred thoroughbred horses.*

# No. 10

## 1937 Mercedes-Benz 540K

### *The Legendary Special Roadster*

**IN EVERY AUTOMAKER'S HISTORY** there are usually half a dozen cars which stand head-and-shoulders above the rest. For Mercedes-Benz, a marque that emerged in 1926 from the merger of two struggling German automakers, Daimler Motors and Benz & Co., those six cars are very easy to name and at the top of the list is the magnificent 1937 Model 540K Special Roadster. A simple analogy—it was Germany's Model SJ Duesenberg.

Mercedes-Benz had already pioneered four-wheel independent suspension with the low-priced Type 170, utilizing a transverse leaf spring in the front and a swing axle design with coil springs in the rear. Mercedes' engineering department refined this design in 1933 for the Type 380, the first production automobile in the world with independent front suspension by means of parallel wishbones and coil springs. The independent rear was a continuation of the proven 170 swing-axle design but fitted with two coil springs per side. The Type 380 was the most advanced automobile in the world, but it had one problem: It was underpowered.

The cars were built on massive box-section frames, which with coachwork averaged well over two tons. At maximum output, 120 horsepower, the beautiful 380s could barely get out of their own way. Even a handful of improved 1934 models with output increased to 140 horsepower, and then 144 horsepower, remained inadequate. The sturdy 3.8-liter engine was simply not powerful enough even with a supercharger. It was at this juncture Mercedes-Benz engineers embraced an established American philosophy: "There is no substitute for cubic inches." Late in 1934, a new 5.0-liter engine was dropped into the 380 and the 500K emerged. They were the same cars but

*The body design and manufacture of the 540K Special Roadster was done at the factory coachworks in Sindelfingen. Only 25 Special Roadsters were produced. This silver car with special white trim was used for the company display at the 1937 Berlin Motor Show.*

*To take full advantage of the 5.4-liter straight eight, 540Ks were equipped with a 4-speed manual transmission. first gear was 3.90:1, second 2.28, third 1.45, and top gear 1:1. This was further improved upon in 1939 when 540K models became available with a new 5-speed transmission offering a 0.80:1 overdrive, or Schnellgang (fast gear). The instruments were of the finest quality and most dashboards were accented with mother of pearl.*

with a new, far more powerful supercharged straight eight beneath the hood. In fact, the early sales catalogs used the same photographs from the 380 brochures!

Considered to be cars of uncommon quality, comfort, and style, the 500Ks immediately proved their mettle in the famous 1934 Tour of Germany endurance test. Covering a distance of 2,195.8 km (approximately 1,364 miles) from Baden-Baden, through Stuttgart, Munich, Nüremberg, Dresden, Berlin (Avus), Magdeburg, Cologne, Nürburgring, and Mannheim, and back to Baden-Baden, the factory 500Ks virtually dominated a field of more than 190 vehicles. Almost overnight the 500K became one of the most desired sports and touring cars in Europe.

In 1937 an even more powerful 5.4-liter supercharged straight eight was introduced as the Type 540K. Both chassis offered coachbuilders an extraordinary platform upon which to mount a custom body. It was composed of two main frame rails, cross braced by one heavy front I-beam, which supported the radiator and independent front suspension mounting; a smaller bolted-in cross member, used to support the rear of the engine and transmission; a large box section cross brace located behind the transmission; and in the rear, two small cross members which served as front and rear supports for the differential.

The frame was tapered at the front, allowing for a narrow radiator, which, along with the engine, was nestled *behind* the front suspension allowing the frame rails, and therefore the bumpers, to extend well past the grille. This gave the cars a longer, leaner appearance regardless of body style.

Despite its tremendous weight, the 500K could accelerate from zero to 62 mph (100 km/h) in under 16 seconds, and in top gear effortlessly attain 100 mph. In the 1930s, any automobile that could achieve triple digits was immediately legendary. With the addition of the 5.4-liter 540K, the mighty Mercedes had reached its zenith. Producing 115 horsepower, increased to a spirited 180 horsepower with the Roots supercharger engaged, Mercedes-Benz fashioned one of the most powerful production automobiles the world had ever seen. After reaching a chest swelling top speed of 106 mph at the famed Brooklands race track during their road test of a 540K, a writer for *The Motor*, one of the leading automotive journals of the day, summarized the experience with these words: "On a fast main-road bend one can hug the kerb at really high speeds in a way which can only be described as comparable to running on rails."

Fitted with the magnificent Special Roadster body, of which only 25 were built, the 540K was unparalleled for its time, with the possible exception of the Model SJ Duesenberg speedsters. One European journalist described the 540K as having "aggressive styling and Teutonic arrogance." It only takes a few minutes behind the wheel to agree. ◆

**PUSH THE ACCELERATOR PEDAL TO THE FLOOR AND THE SUPERCHARGER KICKS IN. THE SOUND IS RAW POWER AND THE SENSATION ALMOST LIKE A SECOND ENGINE IGNITING. THE MECHANICAL CRY OF THE BLOWER IS STARTLING AT FIRST, AND THEN THE ROAD BEGINS TO BLUR UNDER THE TIRES AS MOMENTUM INCREASES.**

*The sweptback styling of the Special Roadster came in two variations, those with an open spare tire and those with a covered spare. The cars also have a rumble seat for two additional and very brave passengers.*

# *No.* 11

## 1886
## BENZ PATENT MOTOR WAGON

### *Driving the First Motorcar*

**THE FORMAL BIRTH OF THE AUTOMOBILE** can be traced back to 1885 when a German engineer named Carl Benz opened the doors of his small Mannheim workshop and rode around the yard in a three-wheeled carriage powered by a single-cylinder, internal combustion engine.

The gasoline engine was not a new idea in the 1880s. Large, stationary engines were in wide use in the latter part of the nineteenth century to power industrial equipment and farm machinery. In fact, Carl Benz had pioneered the development of the stationary engine. It was his conception of a small single-cylinder version that allowed Benz to create a phenomenon in 1885, the motorized carriage.

Though others had tried before him, Benz built the first successful model of its kind powered by a water-cooled, single-cylinder, horizontal engine. The piston and cylinder were oriented fore and aft, and displacement was a mere 954 cubic centimeters, or 58 cubic inches. Output was a trifling three-quarter of a horsepower at just 400 rpm, but it was sufficient enough to impel the lightweight, three-wheel carriage at speeds of up to 10 mph.

The initial trial was in the fall of 1885, whereupon the very first motorized wagon built by Carl Benz stalled and, when restarted, proceeded to snap the drive chain. After making some minor improvements he was ready for another test run a few weeks later. Sitting proudly at the tiller, and with his wife, Bertha, at his side this time, the engine was started by one of his assistants spinning the flywheel. After

*In 1886 a motorized three-wheeler identical to this example claimed the right to be called the first motorcar. Benz was a bicyclist and it seems only natural that a motorized vehicle should be a three-wheeler.*

engaging the chain drive, Carl Benz proceeded to drive the Motorwagen straight into the brick wall of his shop, making this not only the first, but the shortest road test in history.

On January 29, 1886, Carl Benz was granted German patent number 37435 for his invention, the Benz Patent-Motorwagen, regarded today as the first automobile and the source of all that has followed for more than a century.

*Power was taken to the rear wheels by a chain, just like a bicycle. The gear lever is shown just to the left of the seat. Pushing it forward increased speed and pulling it back decreased speed and brought the motorwagen to a complete stop, at least in theory.*

Benz was hesitant to begin production of the Patent Motorwagen while it was still in the developmental stages. His testing had been confined to the road and yard surrounding his workshop. While most would assume that the inventor would be the first to take the Motorwagen out for a long distance trial, it was Carl's wife, Bertha, who would go down in the history books as the first long distance motorist. It happened in the summer of 1888 when Bertha decided to take the second prototype Motorwagen on a journey from Mannheim to Pforzheim to visit her family, a distance of more than 50 miles. With her two sons, Eugen and Richard, she set out at dawn and made the trip in a single day. Wiring her husband—who had been informed of her plans by the note she left for him on the kitchen table which said simply, "We're traveling to Pforzheim to visit Grandma"—she wrote that they had arrived without any significant incidents. For the most part her trip had been uneventful. On the road they encountered two mechanical problems which Bertha tackled with feminine ingenuity. A clogged fuel line was cleared with her hatpin, and when an ignition wire short-circuited she made an insulator out of one of her garters! Except for delays caused by curious passersby, the only other problem was finding fuel. In 1888, of course, the gas station had yet to be invented! The stalwart mother and sons trio reached Heidelberg in time for a midday snack and then pressed on to Wiesloch, where they found an apothecary and purchased benzene to fuel the engine. The town pharmacy, which still exists today, prides itself as having been "the world's first filling station."

The example pictured is one of a handful produced in 1986 by Daimler-Benz engineers using the same type of tools and materials that Carl Benz had at his disposal a century before. The Motorwagens were built to commemorate the 100th anniversary of

THIS IS WHIMSY. YOUR FIRST BICYCLE. YOUR FIRST KISS. SITTING ATOP THE BENCH SEAT AND GRASPING THE TILLER OF THE BENZ PATENT MOTORWAGEN IS TOUCHING THE VERY IDEA OF DRIVING. AT 15 MILES PER HOUR YOU BECOME INTOXICATED WITH THE IDEA THAT THIS IS WHERE IT ALL BEGAN.

the company and are often shown at Concours around the country. Catching a ride in an 1886 Motorwagen is as close as one can come to touching history. Just try to avoid being the guy who has to spin the flywheel to start it! ◆

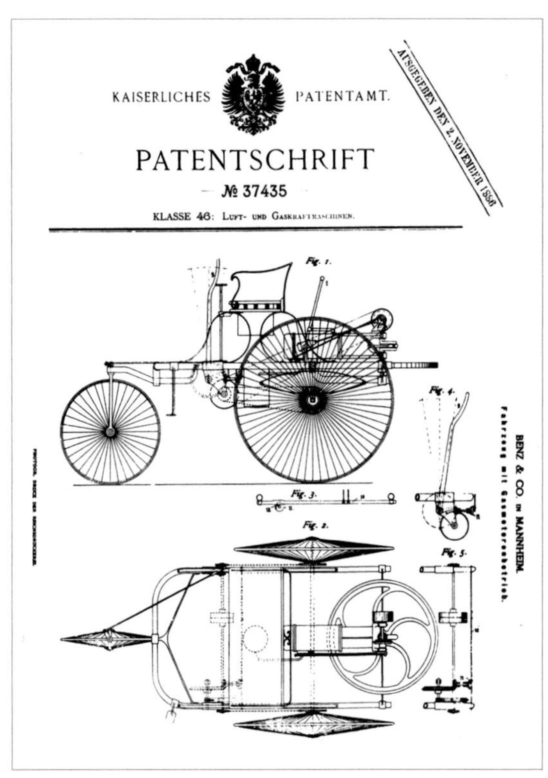
KAISERLICHES PATENTAMT.

AUSGEGEBEN DEN 2. NOVEMBER 1886

PATENTSCHRIFT

— № 37435 —

KLASSE 46: LUFT- UND GASKRAFTMASCHINEN.

BENZ & CO. in MANNHEIM.

Fahrzeug mit Gasmotorenbetrieb.

*The Benz Patent proclaims the 1886 motorwagen as the first motorcar in history.*

*It wasn't much of a powerplant. The 1886 Patent Motorwagen was driven by a single-cylinder engine and started by spinning the massive flywheel. Steering was by tiller, and the only means of braking was the large hand lever acting upon a leather-covered block.*

AHH772

# *No.* 12

## MORGAN SUPER SPORTS THREE-WHEELER

### *The Closest Thing to Flying on the Ground*

**IN 1906, A YOUNG DRAFTSMAN AND ENGINEER** named Henry F. S. Morgan decided to end his career with England's Great Western Railway (he was a mechanical engineer, not the guy who drove the train), and open an automobile garage and motor works in the town of Malvern Link. He was 25 years old, and for the next half century Henry Morgan would build one of Great Britain's most famous sports cars. Of course, at the time, he didn't know it. In fact, Morgan had no intention of becoming an automaker when he opened his garage and began operating a small local bus service.

Morgan's personal car was a three-wheel Eagle Tandem, manufactured by Eagle Engineering & Motor Co. Ltd., in Cheshire. It was a very simple design, inexpensive, and powered by a tiny nine-horsepower, two-cylinder De Dion engine. It wasn't a very good car and it set young Henry to thinking. He could do better.

"It was from his experiences with this machine and a seven-horsepower, two-cylinder car called 'The Little Star' he had the idea of making his own three-wheeler," recalls Henry's grandson Charles Morgan.

### THE NEEDS OF JUST ONE . . . HENRY MORGAN

In 1909, Henry built a lightweight, single-seat, three-wheel cyclecar powered by a seven-horsepower, twin-cylinder Peugeot engine. He used a rigid frame, lightweight

*The red Trike pictured is a 1939 Super Sports model, powered by the Matchless V-twin 40-horsepower engine, which replaced the J.A.P. engine in 1935. The quintessential three-wheeler, this two-seater embodied all the style and unabashed character of the early Morgans. (John Levins collection)*

body, and an independent suspension. It was as simple as the Eagle but a better design. Although he had only built the car for his own interest, as soon as it appeared in public, people began asking where they might obtain one of these wondrous little motorcars for themselves. Thus, with a handful of orders and some money borrowed from his father, Morgan added an extension to his Malvern Link garage and set up machine tools for manufacturing.

He displayed his first single-seat, 961-cubic centimeter J.A.P. powered models (J.A.P. standing for engine designer-builder John Alfred Prestwich), at the 1910 Olympia Motorcycle Show in London. After receiving a patent for his design, Morgan developed a two-seat version which was introduced at the Olympia Motor Show the following year. Morgan's sporty little three-wheelers caught the attention of Harrod's managing director, who was so impressed with the cycle cars that he offered to sell them through the renowned London department store. The first of many high water marks in Morgan's history, these were the only cars ever to appear in the window of the world's most famous retailer.

Morgan found himself eminently successful and with more orders in hand than he could possibly fill. He approached several large manufacturers with an offer to build Morgan cars but everyone turned him down. And that was fortunate. He took it upon himself to expand his facilities and purchase more machine tools, thereby maintaining complete control of his company.

Being a practical man, Henry built his cars as efficiently and inexpensively as possible. One could call his construction methods "frugal," but the cars

*Almost more like a motorcycle with a steering wheel, the interior was laid out for competitive driving with nothing but the essential gauges and a bench seat.*

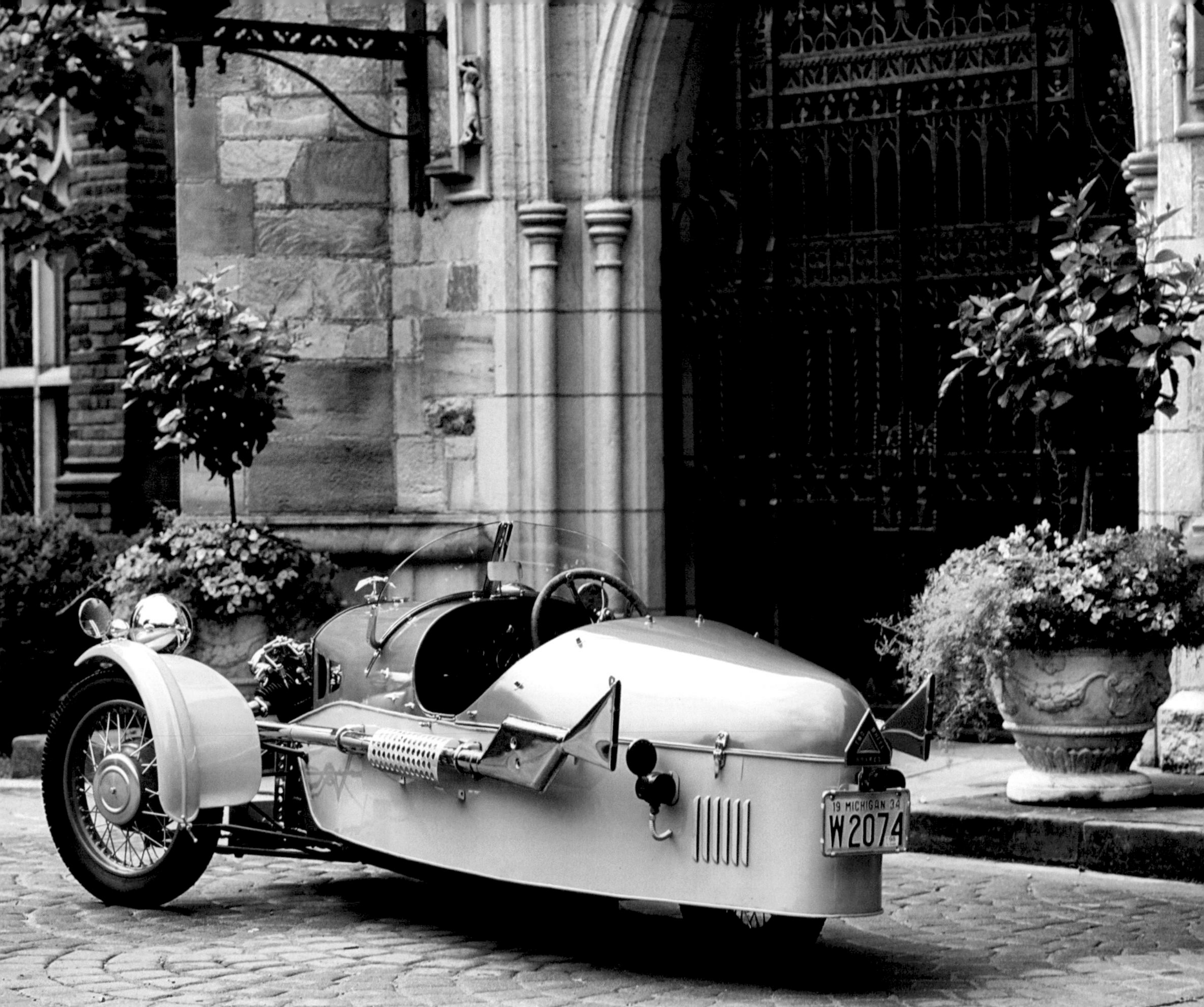


*This 1934 Super Sports is equipped with the air-cooled Matchless V-twin engine and is one of the last Boattail bodies produced. Shortly after 1934, Morgan lowered the exhaust pipes because too many passengers were getting burned while clambering over the side of the car. (Stan Evans collection)*

appealed to buyers just the same. The early two-place, three-wheeled Morgans were built atop a simple ladder chassis with lightweight sheet metal coachwork fashioned around a frame of Belgian ash. This elementary, yet highly efficient layout has become what many motoring authorities consider to be one of the 10 greatest automotive designs of the twentieth century.

## RACING ON THREE WHEELS

Interestingly enough, the simplicity of the car, with its V-twin engine perched precariously in front of the grille, lightweight coachwork, and short wheelbase, also endowed the Morgan Trikes with a remarkable power-to-weight ratio and 90 brake horsepower per ton, which enabled the little vehicles to accelerate as fast as any car being produced. Morgans quickly proved virtually unbeatable in their class, on road, track, and in hill climb competitions. In 1913, Morgans earned more awards for reliability and speed than any other light car in England. As the years passed, Morgans continued to have success upon success in racing, and at Brooklands it was required that Morgans start with a one lap handicap so that other cars in their class might have a chance at winning!

At a price of 85 guineas (approximately $600) the Morgan was not only fast, agile, and affordable, it was also fuel efficient. A Morgan entered in the Cyclecar Clubs Fuel Consumption Trial won the event while averaging 69.4 mpg!

In 1913, the company produced some racing cars with longer chassis, lower seating, and more powerful overhead valve J.A.P. engines. One of the new three-wheelers was entered in the French Grand Prix at

Armiens and handily won against larger four-wheeled European racecars. The competition model became known as the Morgan Grand Prix. By 1914 production had increased to nearly 1,000 cars a year. And then one June day, someone assassinated Austria's Archduke Francis Ferdinand and his wife while they were visiting Sarajevo. A month later all of Europe was at war.

THIS IS FLYING ON THE GROUND. YOU ARE CAUGHT BETWEEN CAR AND MOTORCYCLE AND AIRPLANE, WITH UNUSUAL CONTROLS AND AN ENGINE HANGING OUT FRONT THAT SEEMS ONLY TO BE LACKING A PROPELLER. TWO WHEELS TO STEER AND ONE BEHIND TO MANAGE THE TAIL. YOU ARE EXPERIENCING SOMETHING THAT CANNOT BE FOUND ON FOUR WHEELS, A KIND OF BALANCE THAT LETS YOU SLIDE AROUND CORNERS WITH A SCANT SINGLE WHEEL TRAILING BEHIND. ALL OF THE WEIGHT, ALL OF THE STRENGTH OF THE MORGAN IS IN FRONT.

Although automobile manufacturing was suspended during the war, shortly after the 1918 Armistice, Morgan resumed production, opening a new facility on Pickersleigh Road in Malvern Link. This is still the site of the Morgan Motor Company, which remains family owned to this day.

## LETTING GO OF THE PAST

Henry was by no means a visionary, but he had the foresight to realize that his three-wheelers were quickly going out of style by the mid-1930s, which is ironic since the Great Depression had by then spread to England and all of Europe and inexpensive cars should have been easy to sell. But people wanted four wheels and a more practical design. In December 1935, Morgan announced that the company would begin to produce a more contemporary four-wheeled vehicle. Though not as sporty as the Trikes, the new four-cylinder, four-wheel models quickly grew in popularity. Just as things were looking up, Hitler invaded Poland, and World War II brought another production hiatus for Morgan.

Remarkably, the assembly plant on Pickersleigh Road ended the war virtually unscathed, very well equipped, and ready to resume automobile production in 1945. Though only a few cars were built that year, by 1946 Morgans were being produced at a steady rate and almost exclusively for export. With a flourishing international business, the new 4/4 was in demand; the three-wheelers, however, did not fare as well. There was little export market for the Trikes since other countries did not offer the same tax concessions on smaller vehicles as Great Britain. By 1950, sales were dwindling even for the home market, and in February 1952 Morgan produced its last three-wheeler, marking the end of a 40-year tradition.

Any three-wheeled Morgan makes a great vintage racecar as well as a collectible automobile with a unique character. Even though their values are not remarkable, the fun quotient more than compensates for any lack of return on investment. The cockpit, what there is of it, barely surrounds the driver. The engine is right in front of you. After a few laps in a Morgan Trike it takes about 30 minutes to wipe the grin off your face. World War I flying ace and racecar driver Captain Albert Ball said that driving his Morgan "was the closest thing to flying on the ground." ◆

# No. 13

## Rolls-Royce Silver Ghost

### *The Spirit of Elegant Motoring*

**THE ROAD WE ARE ASCENDING** hasn't changed since the days of Sir William Wallace and his band of rugged Scotsmen, brave souls who went into battle with swords and pikes and bare hands if need be, and afterward dined on haggis. This particular road, aptly named "Rest and be Thankful," is a roughhewn two-mile trail cut through a stunningly beautiful green valley. Even behind the wheel of an automobile you need to rest at the top and you're surely thankful that a tire hadn't blown, the engine overheated, or the car run afoul on the tortuous incline.

Back in June 1907, Claude Johnson, the commercial managing director of Rolls-Royce, Ltd., and a man so instrumental in the company's success that he is often referred to as the "hyphen in Rolls-Royce," drove the very first Silver Ghost in the Scottish Reliability Trial. Known to have a penchant for showmanship, especially when the press was in attendance, he had taken the Silver Ghost up "Rest and be Thankful" a month earlier for a comparison test against a White steam car and had negotiated the final hairpin turn at the hilltop four additional times, twice in reverse, for the benefit of a *London Times* photographer! In June, Johnson and the Silver Ghost completed the 774-mile Scottish Reliability Trial again without incident, winning the Gold Medal for excellence in hill climbing, reliability, and fuel consumption. It was a monumental achievement.

Ninety years later I rode in the very same car and ascended "Rest and be Thankful." For the superbly maintained Silver Ghost, this was the moment of truth. The majority of Rolls-Royce owners, particularly those in Great Britain, do

*Painted a subtle shade of grey with silver-plated fitments, grille shell, and trim, this was the first Rolls-Royce to be called a Silver Ghost. The name was adopted for all 40/50 HP models, but technically this is the only true Silver Ghost in the world.*

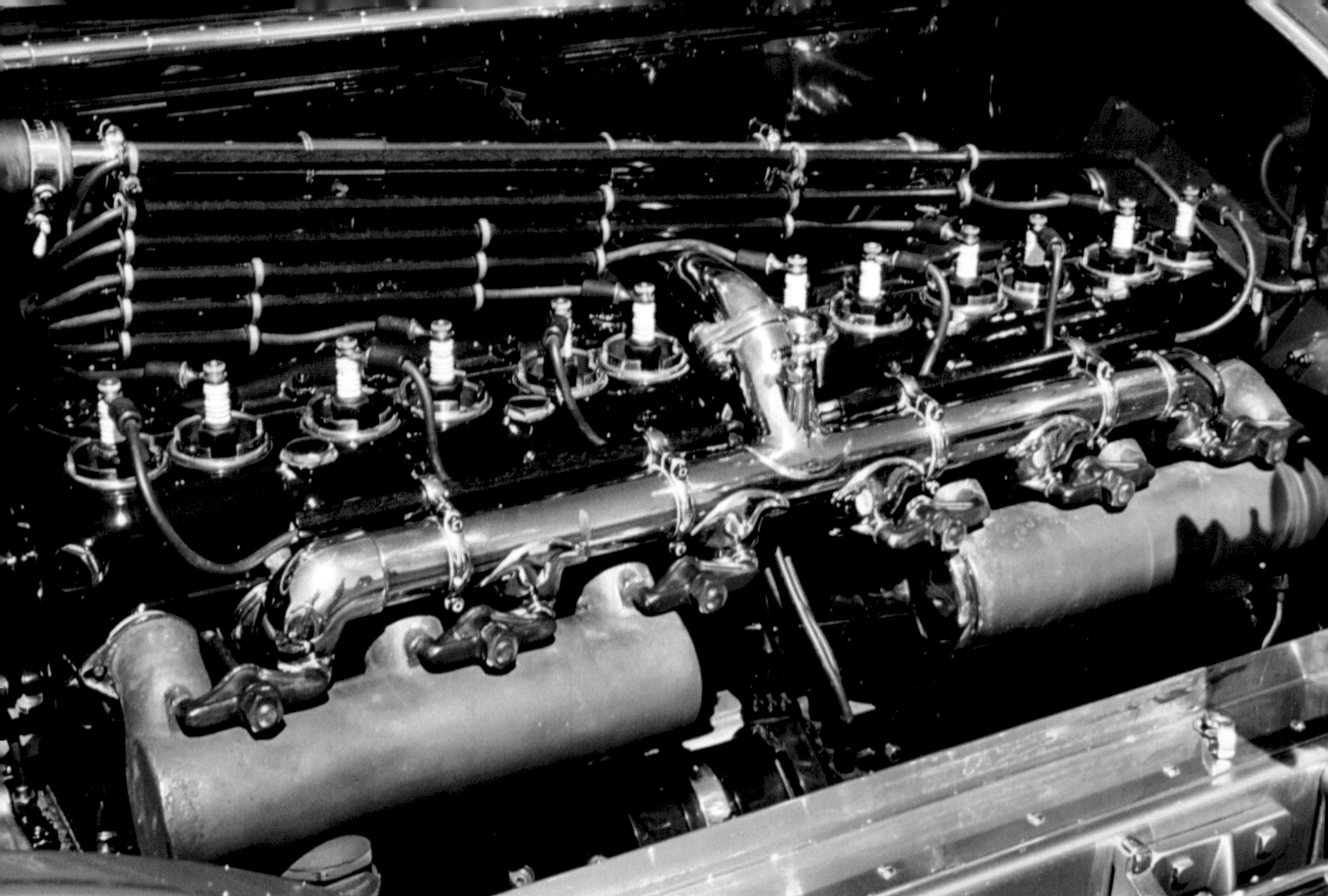

*A century old and still going strong, the Silver Ghost's 40/50 HP six-cylinder engine has recorded 700,000 miles. The Royce-designed engine featured two spark plugs per cylinder and developed 48 horsepower at 1,200 rpm.*

not covet their cars so dearly as to refrain from driving them, even though a Silver Ghost's century-old status and almost irreplaceable coachwork and mechanicals are better suited to a museum than the open road.

On this sunny June day in 1997, I had traveled in the famed '07 Silver Ghost with Richard Charlesworth, then head of Rolls-Royce public affairs, all the way from Glasgow, along the west bank of Loch Lomond, to Tarbet in the Scottish countryside. Here, where the light fidgets through the trees, cities do not exist, and the distance keeps changing, a queue of more than 50 Silver Ghosts, dating from 1907 to 1925, had gathered to follow Charlesworth and Johnson's legendary '07 up "Rest and be Thankful" pass as part of the annual Rolls-Royce Enthusiasts' Club tour.

By modern day standards this rough, ungraded country road would be little threat to a Range Rover or any automobile with four-wheel drive, but these were ponderous old cars, some of them seven feet high at the roofline, riding on narrow rubber tires, wooden spoke artillery wheels, and driven by engines that no matter how well maintained were already 20 years old when George VI was crowned King of Great Britain! This was, as it had been in 1907, a trial of endurance and will, of man and machine, and the conviction of Messrs. Charles Stuart Rolls and Frederick Henry Royce that they did indeed build the best motorcars in the world.

Aside from *the* Silver Ghost, which is owned by Rolls-Royce Ltd., and valued, depending upon who is quoting the figures, at upward of $20 million, the

**DRIVING OR EVEN RIDING IN A SILVER GHOST IS TO LIVE IN A MOMENT THAT WILL NEVER COME AGAIN. CLAUDE JOHNSON'S DEFINITIONS OF THE SILVER GHOST'S PERFORMANCE IN 1907 ARE STILL APPROPRIATE IN THE TWENTY-FIRST CENTURY. AFTER STARTING THE ENGINE WITH ONE OR TWO TURNS OF THE HAND CRANK, THE 7-LITER INLINE SIX COMES TO LIFE WITH A NEAR SILENT CHUFF, RUNNING SO SMOOTHLY THAT THERE IS BARELY A TRACE OF MOVEMENT IN THE BODY AT IDLE.**

average price of a 40/50 HP Silver Ghost participating in the re-creation of the Scottish Tour was close to $1 million. In round figures, that was $70 million worth of cars touring through Scotland.

It's remarkable to go blasting along the motorway at a mile-a-minute in a car that was built when Teddy Roosevelt was president of the United States. But on these roads and in this car, time seemed to have little meaning. The Silver Ghost and the Scottish countryside were the same as they had been in 1907. This particular car was actually the thirteenth 40/50 HP chassis built by Rolls-Royce, serial number 60551, and up until that time the model was simply cataloged by the horsepower rating. It had no name, nor had the famous Spirit of Ecstasy hood ornament yet been created for Rolls-Royce by sculptor Charles Sykes. That wouldn't come until 1910.

## THE NAMING OF GHOSTS

When Claude Johnson saw the beautiful *Roi-de-Belges* Open Touring body for 60551 built for the car in London by Barker, coachbuilders to the Royal Family, he decided it should have a proper name and after some deliberation christened it the "Silver Ghost," which became the popularly accepted designation for all subsequent 40/50 HP models. "Silver, as being pure and hallmarked, and Ghost, as being symbolic of its smooth, silent, effortless movement," wrote Johnson, who commissioned a *repoussé* nameplate for 60551 that still adorns the car's scuttle.

The sheer elegance of this car has made it as timeless as its achievements. Back in July and August 1907, the Silver Ghost established a new record for reliability, covering 15,000 miles, driven day-and-night (except on Sundays) without a breakdown or unscheduled stop. It was indefatigable proof of the car's durability which Johnson had sought to establish. Beginning July 1, Johnson had covered nearly a third of the distance before handing off the car to the Hon. C. S. Rolls, Eric Platford (one of Royce's original apprentices), and Reginald Macready. Johnson took the wheel again to finish the run on Thursday, August 8, 1907, and there among much fanfare and cheers, made a theatrical gesture of turning off the engine for the press. It was done. The world record of 7,089 miles had been broken, better than doubled.

The summer of 1907 had made Rolls-Royce the most talked about automaker in the world and ensured the success of the Silver Ghost for many years to come. Though a century and more than 700,000 miles have passed beneath its wheels, the Silver Ghost remains the essence of Sir Henry Royce's heroic creed: *Quidus recte factum quamuis humile praeclarum.* "Whatsoever is rightly done, however humble, is noble." To drive a Silver Ghost today is one of life's rare little pleasures. ◆

Cisitalia

# No. 14

## 1948 Cisitalia

### *Birth of the Modern Sports Car*

**THE DEFINITION OF A SPORTS CAR,** or to use the even better term "sporting car," has changed many times over the past 100 years. Most examples are clothed with a minimum of coachwork, some little more than a pair of seats on an open chassis. Overall, this was good enough, as most respectable folks drove around

WHEN YOU LIGHT UP THE ANEMIC 50 HORSEPOWER FIAT ENGINE, ITS POWER IS ADEQUATE TO MAKE A CAR THAT COULD BARELY MAINTAIN 65 MPH REACH A SPEED OF 100 MPH. THE SUSPENSION, THOUGH MEAGER IN ITS DESIGN, RESPONDS BETTER BECAUSE THE BODY HELPS STABILIZE THE CAR. THE GEAR SHIFTS ARE SMOOTHER, THE TOP END EASILY OBTAINED. THE CAR IS NOT FIGHTING THE WIND BUT ROLLING THROUGH IT LIKE A HOT KNIFE SLICING A STICK OF BUTTER.

in long wheelbase open tourers, phaetons, sedans, and town cars. Sporting cars were for adventurous young men, playboys, and the foolhardy, the latter group also known as race drivers. The sports car as we regard it today really didn't exist until 60 years ago, when Battista "Pinin" Farina (who in 1961, with the president of Italy's

*The Cisitalia 202 was built atop a simple Fiat 1100S platform and used a Fiat four-cylinder, inline engine. The sleek shape of the body defied the resistance of wind that kept most Fiats under 80 mph and allowed the little 50-horsepower engine to impel a Cisitalia up to 100 mph. The Cisitalia's crowned fenders and oval grille would inspire nearly two decades of Italian sports car styling.*

*The flowing, integrated styling of the Cisitalia rewrote the book on sports car design.*

blessing, would change his family's name to Pininfarina, a combination of his nickname and surname, to match his company) designed the Cisitalia 202 for Italian automotive entrepreneur Piero Dusio.

A wealthy industrialist who had made his fortune during World War II despite the fact that Italy had been on the losing side, Dusio underwrote the development of an entirely new class of racecar immediately after the war. His new automotive company was named Consorzio Industriale Sportivo Italia. The cars, fortunately, went by the contraction C.I.S. Italia, or Cisitalia.

Although his first efforts were toward building a small, affordable fiat-based racecar, the Tipo D46 Monoposto, he soon realized that the same process he was using to build winning competition cars could be applied to a street car—a sports car. Dusio engaged Italian designer Battista "Pinin" Farina to create a new kind of car that could utilize the simple Fiat underpinning and driveline he was using for the D46. Given this free hand and ample finances, Pinin Farina created what he believed would be the next step in automobile design, the envelope body.

When the first pair of Cisitalia 202s appeared at Villa d'Este in 1947, automotive stylists the world over were astounded both by the simplicity of Pinin Farina's design and its completely new approach to body construction. The Cisitalia 202 was the finest expression of Pinin Farina's highly personal style and marked the beginning of the *gran turismo* movement, a sports car body conceived as a single profile rather than as a construct of separate panels. Previously, all automobiles

*Smooth surfaces, a sleek roofline, and crowned rear fenders brought the envelope body into harmony as it wrapped around the back of the car.*

had been based on the traditional prewar blueprint of hood, fenders, body, and trunk being individual components. A perfect example of this design are the popular MG TC and TD models that came from England after WWII. In Italy, where sports car and sports car racing were a national passion, the sleek, envelope styling embodied in the Cisitalia 202 gained momentum. Even though the Cisitalia Granturismo Berlinettas produced in 1947 and 1948 were built atop simple Fiat 1100S platforms and powered by a Fiat four-cylinder developing only 50 horsepower, the sleek Cisitalia body cheated the wind and the cars were able to attain a top speed of 100 mph! The basic design of the Cisitalia would be emulated by European automakers for the next two decades.

The significance of the Cisitalia is exemplified by its selection as the perfect example of sports car design for the 1951 New York Museum of Modern Art exhibition "Eight Automobiles." Since 1972, MOMA has had a Cisitalia displayed as an example of machine art. ◆

*Pinin Farina also redesigned the Fiat 1100S interior for the Cisitalia to appear as sporting as the exterior.*

Stanley

# No. 15

## Stanley Steamer

### *Just Add Water*

**EARLY MOTORISTS HAD TO MAKE** some interesting decisions when purchasing an automobile, including a choice between electric, steam, or gasoline engines—three very different means of propulsion. While the internal combustion engine was being developed in the late 1890s, American and European automakers were also experimenting with electric and steam engines as alternative power sources. In the early years of the twentieth century, the streets of New York, Chicago, and many other major American cities were filled with the pervasive humming of electric cars as they moved almost silently down the boulevard. Electrics were perceived by most people as superior to the vibrating, backfiring, gasoline-powered horseless carriage, and far easier and safer to start than steam-powered automobiles, which required igniting pressurized kerosene to fire the boiler. Electrics, however, were strictly city cars with limited range and equally limited appeal. For the majority of motorists it really came down to a choice between gas and steam, and for a brief time in the automobile's history steam was a very viable alternative. They made sense to most people because steam engines had powered locomotives in America since 1825. It was the Stanley brothers, Francis and Freelan, of Newton, Massachusetts, who put steam power to work in a practical automotive design in 1897.

They were identical twins born in Kingsland, Maine, in 1849, and throughout their lives were of one mind when it came to inventions and business dealings. Among their varied inventions was the dry plate photographic process which they patented in 1893 and subsequently sold to George Eastman. In 1896, shortly after

*In the early 1900s, models such as this 1906 Stanley Steamer Touring were nearly as popular as motorcars powered by gasoline engines. Built on a 100-inch wheelbase, the two-cylinder steam engine produced 20 horsepower and could reach a top speed of 60 mph. (John McMullen collection)*

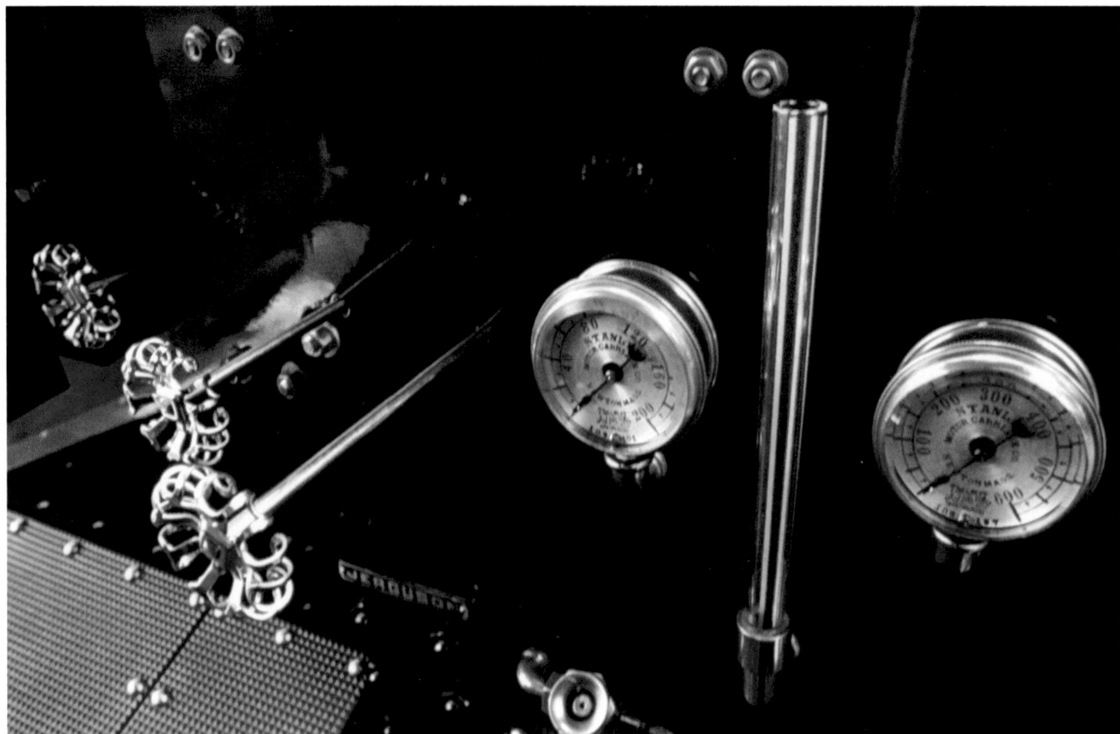

*One needed a complete knowledge of steam-car operation in order to drive a Stanley. There were valves to open and close and adjust in order to control the amount of power delivered to the driveline. There were seven valves to manage overall. In many respects a Stanley was a miniaturized locomotive.*

the Duryea brothers had introduced America's first gasoline motor wagon in Springfield, Massachusetts, the brothers took their profits from Eastman and began to experiment with automobiles, developing an idea they had conceived of a decade before—harnessing steam to power a horseless carriage. They built three prototypes at their shop in Watertown, Massachusetts, in the spring of 1898 and effectively went into business when they sold one of them to a man from Boston for $600. In October, Freelan took another of the prototypes and soundly trounced a field of gasoline-powered motor carriages entered in a one-mile race at the Charles River cycle track near Cambridge. He then proceeded to win a nearby hill-climbing event, which impressed a number of enthusiastic bystanders. By year's end, the Stanley brothers had orders for more than 200 cars.

They set up operations in Newton, Massachusetts, and then sold the entire operation to *Cosmopolitan* magazine publisher John Brisben Walker for a staggering $250,000. Walker and his associate, asphalt manufacturer Amzi Lorenzo Barber, who had literally paved his way to wealth, retained the Stanleys to oversee engineering operations at the Watertown and Newton factories under the newly incorporated name Automobile Company of America. Francis and Freelan had made a killing. Their entire stake in the business had only been $20,000!

Late in 1899, the Automobile Company of America became the Locomobile Company of America, with a capital investment of $2.5 million. The brothers stayed on long enough to fulfill a one-year non-competition agreement they had signed and promptly departed to establish the Stanley Manufacturing Company. With a handsome quarter-million dollar profit, they bought the George E. Whitney

Motor Wagon Company of Boston and began manufacturing steam cars with designs based on their own patents combined with those of Whitney. Two years later they purchased their old Newton works back from Locomobile along with many of their patents for only $25,000 when Walker and Barber parted company on somewhat unfriendly terms.

Back in their old factory, the brothers set up shop under the name Stanley Motor Carriage Co. and began selling rights to their designs to other automakers, including Rollin H. White. By the early 1900s, the two most successful steam-powered automobiles in America were the White and the Stanley. White stayed with steam until 1912, when the company finally converted over to four- and six-cylinder gasoline engines, leaving Stanley as the last major manufacturer of steam-powered automobiles.

And then there was that awful noise. As a Stanley began to boil, the relief valves emitted a sound like a locomotive pulling into Grand Central Station. An early morning firing up would wake everyone within earshot for half a block, adding little to a Stanley owner's popularity in the neighborhood.

The amazing thing was that once underway a Stanley could really perform. It had none of the electric car's speed limitations and, aside from different types of controls, was every bit the equal of a gasoline-powered automobile. The Gentleman's Speedy Roadster, produced from 1906 to 1908, was advertised as the "Fastest Stock Car in the World," and was capable of reaching the then much touted "mile a minute" with its two-cylinder, 20-horsepower steam engine.

## RUNNING OUT OF STEAM

Unfortunately for Stanley and steam cars in general, by 1919 the internal combustion engine had made far greater gains in performance, ease of operation, maintenance, and above all, ignition, following the introduction of the Kettering self-starter in 1912, which all but sounded the death knell for the electric and steam car industries. By 1915 Stanley was delivering fewer than 1,000 cars a year. That number declined to around 600 annually by 1918, when the brothers sold the company to Chicago businessman Prescott Warren. Francis, who was quite content to finally retire, died tragically in an automobile accident that same year. Freelan moved to Colorado where he opened the Stanley Hotel and lived to the ripe old age of 91, running his hotel and telling stories about the Stanley Steamer until he passed away in 1940.

The cars Francis and Freelan had established as early motoring icons were finally run off the road in 1927, when the company's new owners, the Steam Vehicle Corporation of America, succumbed to the design's insurmountable mechanical disadvantages. Despite years of reliable operation and quality manufacturing, Stanleys and their like had finally run out of steam. ◆

THE START-UP PROCESS FOR A STANLEY STEAMER IS LABORIOUS, BUT ONCE YOU HAVE A HEAD OF STEAM THE MOTIVE FORCE IS A TOTALLY DIFFERENT EXPERIENCE THAN A GASOLINE ENGINE AUTOMOBILE. THE POWER JUST KEEPS UNWINDING AS YOU ROLL DOWN THE ROAD. AND WHEN IT COMES TO BLOWING OFF STEAM, NOTHING SOUNDS QUITE LIKE A STANLEY'S HORN, EXCEPT, PERHAPS, AN OLD LOCOMOTIVE.

1963

# *No.* 16

## 1963 Chrysler Turbine

### *The Car of the Future*

**OUTSIDE OF GETTING TO DRIVE ONE** of the turbine-powered GM Firebird concept cars, slipping behind the wheel of a 1963 Chrysler Turbine is as close as any of us will get to being George Jetson.

In 1963, Chrysler's completely redesigned models netted $161.6 million in earnings on more than $1 billion in sales. Much of this was due to Plymouth and Dodge

INSIDE THE CHRYSLER TURBINE THE SOUND IS THAT OF A JET TAXIING DOWN THE RUNWAY. EVERY SENSATION TELLS YOU THIS IS NOT AN AUTOMOBILE, BUT THE STEERING WHEEL BELIES THESE EMOTIONS. AS THE TURBINE SPOOLS UP THE CAR GOES FASTER. THIS REALLY IS FLYING ON THE GROUND.

each delivering nearly half a million new cars. Powering Plymouth's near record sales was the compact Valiant line which accounted for more than a quarter of a million deliveries. Chrysler division production reached 128,997, a healthy indicator that the new body styling was on track.

At Indianapolis, a new Chrysler 300 Sport Series convertible was chosen as the pacesetter for the 47th annual 500-mile Memorial Day Classic, and Chrysler

*From the front, the Turbine's styling wasn't that impressive, but what was under the hood more than compensated.*

*The Turbine body design was done by Chrysler's new chief stylist Elwood Engel, who kept the styling on the conservative side until you came around to the back of the car, which was pure Buck Rogers. What appears to be exhaust nacelles are actually the backup lights. The turbine's exhaust was under the rear of the car.*

stunned the competition by announcing an unprecedented 5-year/50,000-mile power train warranty on all Chrysler cars.

To cap off a remarkable model year, Chrysler debuted an experimental car, the Turbine, a futuristic jet-powered sport coupe designed by Chrysler and bodied in Italy by Ghia, (as Chrysler had done with its concept cars in the 1950s). Unlike most concept cars, the Turbine was a real, fully functioning automobile that was put into limited production for one year, with a total of 50 examples built between October 1963 and October 1964.

## A Subtle Look for an Alternative Future

The Chrysler Turbines were less radically styled than one might imagine and from the front looked very contemporary, almost like a 1962 Ford Thunderbird, an interesting observation since Chrysler's new head of design, Elwood Engel, had come over from the Ford Motor Company to replace chief stylist Virgil Exner. From the rear, Engel's Turbine was something altogether different—different from any car on the road, anywhere. It looked like a jet airplane with taillights!

Although Engel's styling and Ghia's interpretation was anything but over-the-top, the turbine theme was played throughout the car's entire design, from the round turbine bezels surrounding the headlights to the turbine blade wheel covers and turbine-style shaft dividing the interior of the car from front to rear.

The gear selector—Low, Drive, Idle, and Reverse—was mounted in the center console and designed like an aircraft throttle lever. It was surrounded by controls for the lights, windows, and accessories. The feeling in the cockpit was intended to be like that of an aircraft, and when the engine ignited, that is exactly what it felt and sounded like.

The whine of the 130-horsepower turbine spooling up could turn heads for 100 feet in every direction, and on the road there was the distinct trill of air rushing from beneath the car. While it was never so hot that blacktop melted from the exhaust heat (as so many urban myths about the car have proclaimed), the engine did run at 1,250 to 2,000 degrees Fahrenheit, and standing in the turbine's wake at idle was tantamount to being behind a good sized leaf blower on a hot summer day. The engine idled at 22,000 rpm and redlined at a maximum 44,000 rpm. Driving the turbine was definitely an experience.

Although the engine's rated output was only 130 horsepower, it did not translate the same as an internal combustion engine. A little slow off the line, the Turbine clocked 0 to 60 in less than 10 seconds and theoretically had no limit to acceleration, other than the sheer physics of the body design, which kept it down in the neighborhood of 120 mph at full throttle. That was a neighborhood few people were willing to visit in the hand-built Chrysler "loan cars."

Their purpose was to field-test the feasibility of using turbines as an alternative to internal combustion engines. The turbine engines could run on anything from kerosene to jet fuel to 100-proof vodka.

*The 130-horsepower turbine engine wasn't much to look at, but what it lacked in appearance it more than made up for in sound.*

The only problem was fuel economy. At best the cars averaged 11.5 mpg and that performance was a key factor in keeping the Turbine from production.

## A REAL WORLD TEST OF AN OTHERWORLDLY CAR

The 50 Chrysler Ghia Turbines were field tested by 200 selected customers who were given use of the cars for evaluation from 1963 to 1966, at which time they were returned to Chrysler. Most of them were dismantled, and a few, such as this example owned by Frank Kleptz, were sold to private individuals or placed in museums.

Kleptz, who drives his Turbine regularly, still gets a kick out of the sound and the reactions of other motorists. "It was a practical idea in many respects," says Kleptz. "It drives very easily, and since the turbine is simply pushing air, the engine is almost vibration free. If not for the jet-like exhaust, it would almost be silent."

The majority of drivers who tested the Turbines weren't comfortable with the car, felt that it was slower than they expected, and got terrible gas mileage, even though it could run on very inexpensive fuel. Kleptz believes that the car might have been "too odd back then for most people to get comfortable with."

After spending a day in the Turbine, as Frank and I went around Terre Haute, Indiana, looking for photo locations and watching as people stopped in their tracks to look and listen to the car (not to mention the cop who pulled us over), it is hard to believe that anyone could have been disenchanted with the ideal of a jet-powered car in the 1960s. Maybe Chrysler should have had George Jetson test one. ◆

*If there was one thing the Chrysler Turbine lacked, it was flamboyant badging.*

*The interior design was more aircraft- than car-like, with instrument pods and the turbine-styled center console shaft. The controls were also aircraft-like, with the gear selector resembling an engine throttle lever. The turbine-style shaft was used as a styling cue, dividing the car down the middle with bucket seats front and rear.*

# *No.* 17

## 1918 Detroit Electric

### *The Silent Motorcar*

**ALTHOUGH POPULAR IN EUROPE,** electric cars enjoyed their greatest success in the United States, where Fred M. Kimball built the first vehicle of this type in 1888. The first series production was begun by the Electric Carriage and Wagon Company of Philadelphia, which supplied New York City with electric taxis in 1897. Studebaker, in South Bend, Indiana, began building electric cars in 1902, and by 1912 there were more than 20,000 electric vehicles traveling American roads!

THIS IS A SNEAKY CAR. ONCE INSIDE AND UNDERWAY IT IS VIRTUALLY SILENT EXCEPT FOR WHATEVER NOISE THE TIRES MAY MAKE ON THE ROAD. YOU CAN PULL UP ALONGSIDE A CROWD STANDING ON THE CURB AND THEY'LL BE UNAWARE THAT A CAR IS A MERE THREE FEET AWAY.

In the early years of the American automotive industry, electric cars were produced by companies that had no previous ties to the automotive trade. For example, the Baker Motor Vehicle Co. was formed in 1898 by Walter C. Baker, president of the Cleveland-based American Ball Bearing Company. The president of Baker was Rollin H. White of the White Sewing Machine Co., who later became famous as the maker of White Trucks. Baker's first car, a light two-seat electric buggy, was purchased by none other than Thomas Edison, who, when asked if he thought the automobile of the future would be an electric, replied, "I don't think so . . . It would

*How far have we come? In the early 1900s electric cars like this 1918 Detroit Electric Model 75 were efficiently moving through cities at speeds up to 45 mph with a range of almost 90 miles between charges.*

be more likely that they will run by gasoline." Of course, Edison's closest friend was Henry Ford.

The most successful and longest-lived manufacturer of electric cars in America was Detroit Electric. The founding company, Anderson Carriage Manufacturing, was one of the largest carriage makers in the country. In 1907, the Anderson factory in Detroit was reorganized to manufacture Detroit Electric vehicles. Noted for their very manageable steering system and instant start up, they became especially popular with women, making a Detroit Electric the smart thing in which to be seen.

Interiors were stylishly upholstered, and seating in examples such as the Model 75 four-passenger Brougham pictured from the John McMullen collection, resembled a small sitting room, with a plush settee on one side and two smaller seats across from the driver.

*One of the biggest proponents of electric cars was Thomas A. Edison, pictured in the driver's seat of a 1914 Detroit Electric. Edison, however, held out little hope that electrics would survive against gasoline-fueled cars in the future. (Author's collection)*

Although the body was basically carriage-like in design, Detroit Electric employed an innovative shaft drive while most automakers were still using chain drive. The Detroit was the only "Direct Shaft Driven" electric car made. It also had four powerful brakes in two sets acting on the drive wheels to provide an extra margin of safety that the company advertised as being "ten times greater than you will require." The nine different coachbuilt bodies available for the Detroit Electric were constructed of aluminum to lighten the overall weight. As for distance on a full charge, ads quoted the cars as being "more than ample for the day's run." That actually equated to about 90 miles on a charge.

An advertisement in 1911 stated that 14 makers of petrol-engined cars also owned Detroits. Even Henry Ford had a Detroit Electric, as did Thomas Edison and Charles Edison, whose nickel-steel batteries were available at extra cost on Detroit Electrics.

Sales of Detroit Electrics, and electric vehicles in general, began to decline after World War I. In 1919 the company was renamed the Detroit Electric Car Co. and though commercial Detroits ceased production in 1927, passenger cars continued to be built to special order. Town carriage styling similar to the 1910 pattern was still being offered as late as 1930, though very few were made after 1935. In 1939, with demand for electric vehicles almost nil, the firm closed its doors.

From the 1890s through the 1930s there were more than 300 different electric car makes in the United States alone. But what had begun as one of the most successful industries in the world at the turn of the last century simply went out like a light in 1939. One can only imagine how far electric car technology would be today if the original companies like Detroit Electric had survived. ◆

*The Detroit Electric Brougham seated four, two on a large bench seat and two in small, plush chairs. The driver sat in the left rear of the compartment. A floor pedal under the driver's seat was used to select forward or reverse. The driver had two levers with which to operate steering and gear change, although the Detroit had no actual gears. Instead, each increment in the four-speed increased electric power to hasten the car's pace, and all four speeds worked in either forward or reverse. Both the tiller steering arm and shifter folded out of the way for easier entry and exit.*

# *No.* 18

## FERRARI 410 SUPERAMERICA

### *Pininfarina's Favorite*

**IT IS SAFE TO SAY THAT HAD IT NOT BEEN** for the wealth and enthusiasm of American sportsmen like Briggs Cunningham, who purchased the first Ferrari imported into the United States and won the first race in which it was entered at Watkins Glen, New York, in 1949, there would likely be no Ferrari today. The very success of the company in the late 1940s and early 1950s was founded on the sales of sports and racing cars to Americans.

By the early 1950s, the United States was Ferrari's most lucrative market, and

THIS WAS A LUXURY CAR BY FERRARI STANDARDS. YOU'RE SURROUNDED BY HAND-SEWN ITALIAN LEATHER AND PLUSH CUT PILE CARPETING, AND MATCHING TRIM, BUT UNDER THE HOOD IS A V12 THAT WILL TAKE YOU TO SPEEDS THAT FEW COULD EXPERIENCE BACK IN THE 1950S.

the ultimate Ferrari road and racecar of the early fifties was the 410 Superamerica. By 1956, Sergio Pininfarina had already designed several significant cars for Ferrari but the 410 Superamerica was the most significant. Only nine examples were produced by Pininfarina in this original style, including the car pictured, 0423 SA, but the styling cues created for the 410 inspired Ferrari designs for nearly a decade.

*The 410 Superamerica body surrounded Ferrari's bold oval grille with high-crowned fenders stretched into one fluid line along the length of the body, wrapping into a pronounced kick-up just behind the doors.*

*Chrome was a Ferrari's best friend in the 1950s. The pronounced oval grille of the 410 Superamerica was balanced by the use of brightwork around the functional side vents (the first use of side vents on a road car), on the decklid, and the front and rear bumper treatments.*

Explains Sergio Pininfarina, "It [was] not a matter of styling the car in one way more than another but designing the right type of car for the [American] market. The car is not always moving, and it must be something that the driver enjoys just looking at. And then people, ordinary people on the street, look at the car also, and they must see something special. It must have a definite personality that shows to the public distinctively that this is a Ferrari."

The styling of the first 410 Superamericas formed the basis for the design of such memorable sports cars as the 250 GT PF (Pinin Farina) coupes and the legendary 250 GT Berlinetta Tour de France. It would also influence the 250 GT Spyder California, another Ferrari built for the American market.

The 410 Superamericas were powered by the same Lampredi-designed V12 engines that Ferrari had used to win the 24 Hours of Le Mans, the Buenos Aires 1000km, and the PanAmericana roadrace. Wanting to offer an engine that had the swept volume Americans expected in a sports car, Ferrari increased the V12 used in the 410 to nearly 5.0 liters, a number that easily turned heads when converted to cubic inches—302 of them. Mixing air and fuel through a trio of twin-choke 42DCZ Weber downdraft carburetors, with a compression ratio of 8.5:1, the 60-degree V12 delivered 340 horsepower at 6,000 rpm, and versions produced in 1958 and 1959, with 9:1 compression, developed a staggering 400 horsepower at 6,500 rpm. Ferrari limited production of the 410 Superamerica, the most powerful road car yet put into the hands of its clientele, to one per month.

In 1956, the 410 Superamerica sold for an astounding $16,800. By comparison, a Cadillac Fleetwood 75 limousine, the most expensive American car built that year, sold for $6,240. Even in 1957, when Cadillac introduced the ultra luxury Eldorado Brougham, it was more than $3,000 *less* than a Superamerica. The 410 was then, as it is now, one of the world's most exclusive sports cars. ◆

*The interior of the 410 Superamerica was more finely detailed than that of any previous Ferrari model. The car utilized a 4-speed synchronized (Porsche-type) transmission. The most disconcerting feature of the transmission was that, on the majority of cars, first gear was found forward and to the right, and fourth was back and to the left.*

# *No.* 19

## 1958 DUAL-GHIA

### *Hollywood Status*

**DESPITE A QUALITY PRODUCT,** by the early 1950s Chrysler had been burdened with what some pundits called a "stodgy, old-man's-car image" and Chrysler was banking on the company's new chief stylist, Virgil Exner, to turn things around. A conceptualist who could see beyond the warmed-over prewar designs being popularized by other Detroit stylists, Exner was also shrewd enough to know he would require outside assistance to create this new image for Chrysler. He decided to have his prototypes hand-built and far from the Detroit environment by metal crafters who could capture the subtlety of every line. After World War II Chrysler employees were sent to Italy to teach American manufacturing techniques to Fiat managers and employees as part of the Marshall Plan for European recovery. While Americans were teaching Italian automakers how to build cars "Detroit-style," they were learning a great deal about the Italian automotive industry, including its guild of small, family-owned *carrozzeria*. Exner forged an alliance with Ghia in Turin, Italy to build his "Idea Cars," concepts that would take Chrysler a generation ahead of Ford and GM in styling. In 1955, Exner's "100 Million Dollar Look" put Chrysler at the forefront of American automobile design.

Exner had set the stage for Chrysler's styling renaissance back in 1949. "Our cars are not of the future," he said, "but new idea cars exploring excitingly new workable areas of styling and design." The bold, new Chrysler models of the 1950s

---

*Owned and restored by Mike Stowe of Great Lakes Motor Works in Boyne City, Michigan, this is the finest Dual-Ghia known. Among the people who took interest in the car's restoration was Tom Gale, retired Chrysler vice president of design, who came up with the distinctive color scheme for the body and interior. The color is "Silk Khaki," which changes intensity depending upon the light, varying from gray green to silver gray. The car's wheelbase measures 115 inches.*

*The deep-dish steering wheel was from a Chrysler, the dash knobs from a Plymouth, the gauges from Dodge. The interior, however, was purely Italian in design, with a large instrument pod and luxurious hand-sewn leather upholstery. The balance of gauges in the center of the dash relayed generator charge, fuel level, oil pressure, and coolant temperature. The radio was a Philco Touch-Tuner. The Dual-Ghias were all equipped with a Chrysler PowerFlite two-speed automatic transmission with the shifter mounted on the center tunnel.*

evolved from Exner's Chrysler Specials, all of which had wowed the public at the nation's major auto shows as part of Chrysler's "New Worlds In Motion" exhibit. It was the experimental Firearrow, however, that would result in one of the most interesting and exclusive coachbuilt cars of the 1950s.

The Dual-Ghia came about at the same time the Nash-Healey and Chevrolet Corvette were setting the American road on fire, and just before the debut of the 1955 Ford Thunderbird. So the idea of Chrysler building a sports car wasn't too far-fetched, except that the company had no intention of getting into the sports car business in the 1950s. While this should have been the end of the story, it was just the beginning.

## TURNING A CONCEPT INTO REALITY

Eugene Anthony Casaroll, founder of Dual Motors Corporation in Detroit, had made his fortune prior to WWII developing the design for a commercial car hauler and establishing the first company to transport

*Body panels were hand-formed from steel shaped over aluminum dies, then butt-welded together into a unit body, which in turn was welded to a modified Dodge chassis. The compound curves of the car were too difficult for mass production. A total of 117 cars were built between 1956 and 1958, including prototypes.*

vehicles from the automaker's assembly plants to their dealerships. Up until then, cars had been delivered by rail to depots or picked up at the factory and driven to the dealerships. At its height, Casaroll's Automobile Shippers, headquartered in Detroit, had a fleet of 130 car haulers in operation.

Realizing that Chrysler had no intention of building the Firearrow, Casaroll decided to produce an Italian-bodied sports car with an American driveline. Something similar to what Nash had done with the Pininfarina-bodied Healeys, but in a more luxurious, *gran turismo* (GT or grand touring) style. Casaroll asked Chrysler for permission to develop the Firearrow on his own as a production car. To his surprise, Chrysler wholeheartedly agreed with the idea.

The transatlantic relationship between Chrysler and Ghia had already brought about a series of limited production models closely resembling Exner's 1952 Chrysler Special, which were being sold exclusively in Europe by Société France Motors as the Ghia GS-1. This was a shrewd business decision because every Ghia-bodied car built was essentially a sale for Chrysler, since Dodge chassis, engines, drivelines, and Chrysler components were being used in their manufacture. The Dual-Ghias would add to the sales tally while at the same time providing Chrysler with a high-profile sports car image for the American market.

Casaroll was introduced to Ghia's director, Luigi Segre, who was equally intrigued by this idea, and almost overnight, Casaroll found himself in the driver's seat of his Dual Motors Corporation.[1] In Italy,

1. Dual Motors Corporation had been formed by Casaroll to manufacture heavy-duty twin-engine trucks for the Air Force during World War II, along with twin-engine stationary power plants for the Corps of Engineers, thus the origin of Dual Motors, and the Dual-Ghia name.

*The standard Dual-Ghia engine was a 315-cubic-inch Dodge V8 with wedge combustion chambers. Equipped with a four-barrel carburetor, it delivered 230 horsepower. Those desiring a bit more go in their Dual-Ghia could opt for the 260-horsepower, 315-cubic-inch Chrysler Hemi for an additional $100.*

Ghia chief stylist Giovanni Savonuzzi was assigned the job of refining the Firearrow prototype into a production car, which made its debut in March 1955 as the Firebomb. And it was. The car was beautiful but fraught with engineering and manufacturing problems. Casaroll and his team went back to the drawing board, quite literally, and a year later the Dual-Ghia made its debut.

## THE DUAL-GHIA

Savonuzzi's changes to the Firearrow had been spectacular, retaining the essence of the concept car but adding the character and practicality necessary for a production vehicle. The Firearrow's pillar-free windscreen had been replaced by a Dodge windshield, a small but attractive fin added to the rear fender line, and 1956 Dodge bumpers skillfully blended into the lines of the hand-formed steel bodywork. The driveline and suspension were a combination of Dodge and Chrysler parts, making the Dual-Ghia a true American-Italian hybrid, inspiring the Dual-Ghia emblem of crossed American and Italian flags.

To assemble the cars, Dodge frames were first shipped to Turin for coachwork, which took 1,300 man hours to complete, then shipped back to Detroit, where the assembly team at Dual Motors spent another 200 hours per car attaching the suspension, wheels, engine, and drivetrain.

The standard Dual-Ghia engine was a 315-cubic-inch Dodge V8 with wedge combustion chambers. Equipped with a four-barrel carburetor, it delivered

THE DUAL-GHIA IS THE BEST OF BOTH WORLDS, POSTWAR HORSEPOWER WITH OLD WORLD COACHBUILT ELEGANCE. THE HEMI ENGINE BELTS OUT ENOUGH POWER TO MAKE THIS A VERY FAST CAR BUT AT HEART, IT IS A GRAND TOURING CAR THAT LONGS TO BE DRIVEN ON OPEN ROADS WITH THE TOP DOWN AND THE WIND WHIPPING AROUND THE WINDSHIELD. SIT BACK, TUNE IN A DEAN MARTIN OR FRANK SINATRA SONG ON THE RADIO, AND HEAD FOR PALM SPRINGS, CALIFORNIA.

230 horsepower. Those desiring a bit more go in their Dual-Ghia could opt for the 260-horsepower, 315-cubic-inch Chrysler Hemi for an additional $100. Both engines were coupled to the Chrysler Power-Flite 2-speed automatic, an unintentional and ironic similarity to the Corvette, which had been saddled with a 2-speed automatic. With the big Hemi V8 under its hood there was never a discouraging word about the Dual-Ghia's Power-Flite automatic.

The lavishly appointed interior was typical of Italian sports cars from the 1950s, with a large instrument pod and two big gauges, one of which was a speedometer taken from the Dodge parts bin. Since Dodge didn't have a tachometer, and a sports car needed one, Ghia fabricated a tach to match the Dodge design. Both were framed by a deep dish Chrysler steering wheel fitted with the Dual-Ghia emblem. Upholstery was all hand-sewn leather in the Italian tradition, luxurious and supple to the touch.

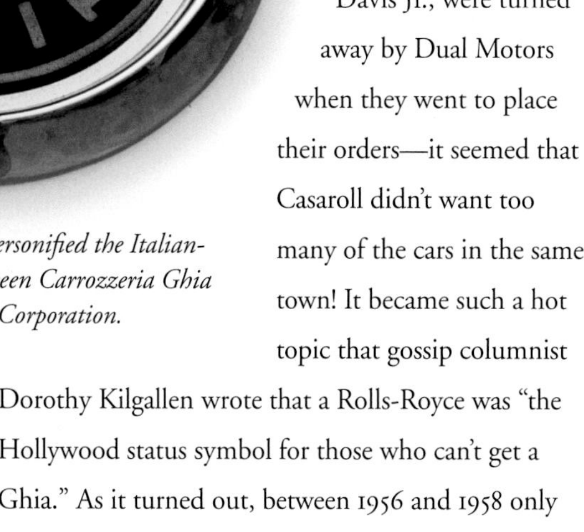

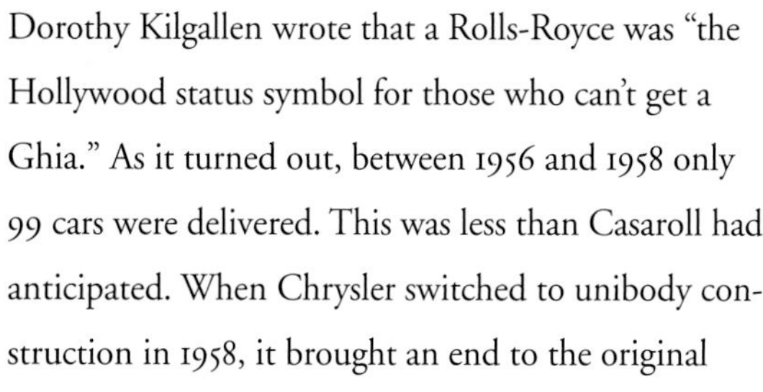

*The Dual-Ghia emblem personified the Italian-American relationship between Carrozzeria Ghia and Dual Motors Corporation.*

The Dual-Ghias were among the most expensive automobiles sold in America; at $7,646 they were about $1,000 more than a 1957 Cadillac Eldorado Biarritz. They immediately struck a cord with the Hollywood elite and the register of early owners included Frank Sinatra, Peter Lawford, Eddie Fisher, Debbie Reynolds, Lucille Ball, Glenn Ford, composer and singer Hoagy Carmichael (the second owner of the car pictured), and composer David Rose. Interestingly, Rat Packers Dean Martin and Sammy Davis Jr., were turned away by Dual Motors when they went to place their orders—it seemed that Casaroll didn't want too many of the cars in the same town! It became such a hot topic that gossip columnist Dorothy Kilgallen wrote that a Rolls-Royce was "the Hollywood status symbol for those who can't get a Ghia." As it turned out, between 1956 and 1958 only 99 cars were delivered. This was less than Casaroll had anticipated. When Chrysler switched to unibody construction in 1958, it brought an end to the original coachbuilt Dual-Ghia design. ◆

# *No.* 20

## 1950 Ferrari 166 Mille Miglia

### *The Source Ferrari*

**AT THE AGE OF 48, LUIGI CHINETTI** already had a brilliant racing career, having won the 24 Hours of Le Mans twice, first in 1932 and again in 1934. In 1949, as the sole importer of Ferrari in the United States, he returned to Le Mans and won his third 24 Hours driving the new 166 MM Touring Barchetta, the first Ferrari ever to win the event. At the time, Chinetti was the only three-time winner of the race. His co-driver, Lord Selsdon of Scotland (Peter Mitchell-Thompson), clocked only 20 minutes behind the wheel, with Chinetti driving more than 23 of the 24 hours! Following the race, Lord Selsdon purchased the car from Chinetti. The victory at Circuit de la Sarthe was not as important to Chinetti as the publicity it generated for the fledgling Ferrari enterprise in which Chinetti had placed both his money and his faith.

### CREATING A FERRARI ROAD CAR

A year before the Le Mans victory, the Ferrari factory in Italy was producing only racecars, which Chinetti was selling to clients in the United States and France. But he knew full well that racecars alone would not sustain the company. Ferrari needed a model that could be both road car and racecar. He finally convinced Enzo Ferrari to produce such a vehicle as the sales of sports cars, which Ferrari had no interest in building at the time, would bring in money to support the racing effort and promote the company's image. When Ferrari saw the logic in this he turned to an old

*Over time, the basic Barchetta design shown on this 1950 model was modified to accommodate a variety of wheelbases, including the original 86.6-inch chassis used for the 166 MM and 195 S, the later 88.6-inch 166 MM chassis, the 212 Export, and the 95.2-inch wheelbase 340 America. (Chip Connor collection)*

friend, Carlo Felice Bianchi Anderloni of Carrozzeria Touring, and asked him to design a suitable sports car body for the Tipo 166 racecar.

One of Italy's oldest design houses, Touring was established in 1926 and was renowned for designing and building some of the most exciting sports and racecars of the 1930s. Enzo's relationship with Touring dated back to the years when he had managed the Alfa Romeo race team, Scuderia Ferrari, and Anderloni had designed and produced the majority of bodies for Alfa. In 1948, the first sports car design ever shown on a Ferrari chassis, the 166 MM Touring Barchetta, made its debut at the Turin Salon. More than half a century later it is still among the most admired of all Ferrari models.

The Barchetta's styling was based in part on another legendary sports car designed by Touring, the 1940 BMW 328 Spyder. The 166 MM design introduced sleek, swept-back lines, a long hood, short rear deck, and an aggressive oval grille which was to become a Ferrari styling cue for many years. The Barchetta's design would be copied, or as some say, would "influence" other sports cars including the AC Ace and AC Bristol, which evolved into the Shelby Cobras of the 1960s.

The styling of the Barchetta (which in Italian means small boat), was a significant break with traditional sports cars of the day. Wrote Anderloni: "We were attempting to individualize the Ferrari and

*Opposite. The* Superleggera *hood emblem indicated that the car was of Carrozzeria Touring's exclusive lightweight construction. The* Superleggera *name became as well recognized as that of the Milanese coachbuilder.*

*Below. The interior of the 166 Barchetta features beautiful hand-sewn leather upholstery and trim. Its simplicity of design was purely race bred. The cars were considered luxurious, or Lusso, when given the full interior treatment.*

Ferrari

*The aggressive body was set atop the patented* Superleggera *welded tubular steel frame on a wheelbase of 2,200 millimeters (86.6 inches). Track measured 1,270 millimeters (49.8 inches) front and 1,250 millimeters (49.2 inches) rear.*

not to copy one of the many 'Spider' two-seat sports cars in circulation . . . the results were obtained by overturning the strictest canons of sports car design, which was normally wide at the bottom, narrow at the top, and close to the ground." Overturning was an apt choice of words as the Barchetta had its maximum width just over halfway up the side and visibly high off the ground, just the opposite of contemporary designs.

Officially, the cars were cataloged as the 166 Mille Miglia or MM, a name chosen in honor of Ferrari's 1948 victory in the grueling thousand-mile Italian road race; Barchetta, however, was readily used by everyone, even Ferrari.

## THE BODIES BEAUTIFUL

The Touring coachwork incorporated the firm's exclusive *Superleggera,* or super-light, construction method of small, lightweight steel tubes to which the body panels were attached. Most of the 166 MMs were painted a deep, fiery red, which became another Ferrari tradition. Virtually every Barchetta was a racecar, whether a competition model powered by the 140-horsepower Export V12 or the more luxurious Lusso, with the 110-horsepower Inter V12.

The handcrafted bodies were attached to a welded tubular steel framework and then mounted

NOTHING COMES CLOSER TO EXPERIENCING THE GLORY DAYS OF ROAD RACING IN THE 1950S THAN DRIVING A FERRARI 166 MM. THE V12 UNWINDS AT HIGH PITCH, THE EXHAUST ECHOES IN THE AIR, AND THE THINLY DISGUISED RACECAR BODY TREMBLES AS THE 166 ROARS DOWN THE ROAD. IN A LUSSO (LUXURY MODEL) LEATHER IS USED TO DECORATE THE INTERIOR PANELS BUT THE COMPETITION CAPABILITIES ARE THE SAME.

on the Barchetta's short 2,200-millimeter (86.6-inch) wheelbase chassis. The front suspension was Ferrari's independent A-arm design, supported by a single transverse leaf spring; the rear, a live axle with semi-elliptic springs and parallel trailing arms on each side. Easily the fastest sports car in the world at the time, Ferrari recorded more than 80 overall or class victories between April 1948 and December 1953. Enzo Ferrari had established his reputation as a sports car builder, even if he didn't want one.

Throughout the 1950s and even into the 1960s, whenever the Ferrari name was mentioned, the image that most often came to mind was that of the 166 MM Barchetta. The last one was built by Touring in 1952, mounted on the newer 212 chassis and presented to Henry Ford II as a gift from Enzo Ferrari. ◆

*Touring's 166 MM Barchetta overturned the canons of sportscar design with the width of the body being just over halfway up the sides, like the hull of a speed boat.* Barchetta *means small boat.*

# No. 21

## 1965 Shelby 427 Cobra

### *British Brawn, American Power*

**CARROLL SHELBY HAD HIS FILL OF FEATHERS** by the early fifties when the Texas chicken rancher found his true calling behind the wheel of a second hand MG TC. He had a natural skill for racing. Carroll was aggressive and intuitive; he drove hard and won a lot of races by the late fifties, working his way up to bigger and faster sports cars until the day he caught the attention of Brit John Wyer, Aston Martin's team manager. Wyer signed him up and the tall Texan with incredible driving skills became only the second American race driver in history to win the 24 Hours of Le Mans, bringing the David Brown "DB" Aston Martins worldwide recognition in 1959. What Carroll didn't mention at the time was that he had a bad heart. Not only had he beaten the other drivers he had cheated death, popping nitroglycerin tablets to ease the angina pains racking his chest as he manhandled his Aston Martin around the demanding 8.47-mile Circuit de la Sarthe. Shelby ended his racing career a year later by clinching the USAC driving championship. Rather than hanging it up and returning to his Texas farm to pick up where he left off , Shelby reckoned that, "If I can't race cars, then I can build 'em." Five years later, the Ford-sponsored Shelby American race team won the World Manufacturer's Championship.

Ford can thank General Motors for the title, at least indirectly. Two years after winning the championship he had gone to GM with his "idea" to put a Chevy V8 under the hood of an AC Ace roadster manufactured in England by AC Cars. The guys on the fourteenth floor mulled it over and figured it would take sales away from the Corvette, which was probably true. What they didn't figure on was Carroll

*For 1965, Shelby, AC cars, and Ford formed an alliance that resulted in the most powerful sports car of its time, one that even Ferrari could not defeat. The most desirable is the 427 SC version, distinguished by its riveted hood and aggressive stance. (Bruce Meyer collection)*

In all of American automotive history no car is as compelling to drive, and drive hard, as a 427 Cobra. It is pure adrenalin crafted in aluminum and steel. The great Ford V8 beckons you, dares you to use it. The gearbox and clutch put you in command of raw, unrestrained horsepower. Depress the heavy-duty clutch, work the shifter, and get ready to go fast. The Cobra doesn't have a touring mode. Once you let the clutch out, you're at the top of the rollercoaster ride.

going across town to Ford with the idea, and Ford needed a car to compete with the Corvette. He got an introduction from *Hot Rod* magazine editor Ray Brock, and Ford was willing to give the idea a shot. The company had nothing competitive to the Corvette on or off the race track.

Lee Iacocca was in the process of reshaping Ford's image in the early 1960s and prosperity was about to fall into Shelby's lap. Shortly after Iacocca became vice president and general manager of Ford, his boss, Henry Ford II, said he "wouldn't be opposed to a factory racing program in full public view."

Ford sent a financial analyst named Ray Geddes out to Southern California to evaluate the Shelby prototype, which was now fitted with a Ford V8. He was introduced to the prototype AC Cobra and

*Wide Goodyear 8.15" x 15" tires and a race-tuned four-wheel independent suspension combined with the power of the 427-cubic-inch V8 made the Cobra almost unbeatable in sports car competitions.*

*The Ford 427 V8 engine used in the Shelby Cobras unleashed 390 horsepower through a 4-speed, all-synchromesh gearbox and Salisbury, limited-slip differential.*

handed the keys for a test drive. Geddes sat behind the wheel, started the engine, shifted into first gear, and almost drove it into a telephone pole. It was the fastest car he had ever been in. "Left Geddes pretty damned impressed," said Shelby. Geddes told Henry Ford II that the company should make Shelby Enterprises a separate company, provide dealers, engines, technical assistance, and above all else, the financing to get the operation up and running as quickly as possible. The Texan was about to go head-to-head with GM's tempestuous Zora Arkus-Duntov, who was preparing to launch the all-new Corvette Sting Ray, a car that GM had assumed would be virtually uncontested in SCCA and sports car competition.

The 289 Cobras were formidable competitors in the hands of drivers like Dave MacDonald and Ken Miles, but during the Bahamas Speed Week in 1964, Duntov's Corvettes trounced the Cobras. Ford had been outgunned by more powerful Chevy V8s, and Shelby was already plotting a solution before the dust had settled in Nassau.

At Sebring in October 1964, Shelby American entered a Ford Cobra prototype, CSX 2166, powered by a 427-cubic-inch V8. This was a prelude to the cars that would begin appearing at race tracks and on dealer showroom floors by 1965. The new 427 Cobra featured a tube frame, coil spring chassis, and a light-alloy body design that looked downright angry. The Shelby 427 Cobras became the most formidable sports cars of the 1960s. Not only did they leave the Corvettes in the dust, on July 4, 1965, Shelby's 427 Daytona Cobras defeated Ferrari to claim the World Manufacturer's Championship title, fulfilling a prediction made a year before by Carroll: "Ferrari's ass is mine." Subtlety was never a characteristic of Shelby or his cars. ◆

300-SL

# *No.* 22

## 1954 Mercedes-Benz 300 SL Gullwing Coupe

### *Racing Improves the Breed*

**IT IS ONE OF AUTOMOTIVE JOURNALISM'S** most popular clichés that racing improves the breed, but it is also one of the truest statements ever made when it comes to automobiles and their engineering. Luigi Chinetti forced Enzo Ferrari to recognize this in the early 1950s but in quite the opposite fashion as Ferrari was then only building racecars. Out of the racecars came the road cars, and one fed upon the other, the profits from road car sales funding racecar development and the improvements in racecars leading to better road cars. When Mercedes-Benz returned to sports car racing in 1952 with the 300 SL, the company had been inspired by the 1951 Jaguar C-Types, a reworking of the XK-120 road cars. The championship '52 Mercedes racecars encouraged the company to build a 300 SL sports car in 1954, a model that would never have seen the light of day had it not been for the racecars.

With the European championship under its belt and a victory in the 1952 Carrera Panamericana, the "gullwing Mercedes" was one of the most talked about racecars in the world. With a little added persuasion from U.S. importer Max Hoffman, the company gave chief engineer Rudolf Uhlenhaut and his designers the go-ahead to turn the 300 SL racecar into a production sports car. This was late in 1952 and the car had to be ready for introduction as a 1954 model! Doing the seemingly impossible, however, was Uhlenhaut's specialty. He had designed the racecar in less than a year!

The production version was based on physical presence. The car captured the look and, to some extent, the performance of the SL racecars but embraced it in the

*The sleek, aerodynamic form of the 300 SL was derived from the original racecar design created in 1952. Refined for the street by stylists Karl Wilfert and Paul Braiq, the 300 SL was voted "Sports Car of the Century" in 1999.*

THIS WAS NOT A COMFORTABLE CAR TO DRIVE IN LESS THAN IDEAL WEATHER. TEMPERATURES INSIDE THE ENCLOSED COCKPIT CAN BECOME UNPLEASANT IN HOT WEATHER. VENTILATION IS ADEQUATE BUT SINCE THE WINDOWS DON'T GO DOWN THERE ISN'T MUCH OF IT. DRIVE THE 300 SL HARD AND IT WILL REWARD YOU WITH EXHILARATING PERFORMANCE, ONE OF THE FASTEST FROM ZERO TO 60 MPH OF ITS DAY AND EASILY CAPABLE OF BETTER THAN 125 MPH. SOLID, QUIET (THANKS TO WILFERT), BUT NO LESS AWKWARD TO GET IN AND OUT OF THAN THE 1952 RACECAR, CLAMBERING OVER THE HIGH DOOR SILL CREATED BY THE CAR'S TUBULAR FRAME. ONCE INSIDE, YOU ARE SURROUNDED BY THE MOST EXOTIC GERMAN SPORTS CAR OF THE 1950S.

handcrafted luxury for which Mercedes was recognized. The car had to be altered considerably to meet production requirements, yet the similarities between the racecars that had swept the 1952 season and the sports cars that would sweep Americans off their feet two years later was unmistakable.

## FROM RACECAR TO ROAD CAR

The most significant mechanical difference between the 1952 competition cars and the production SL was the fuel intake system. The competition cars used three Solex 40 PBJC downdraft carburetors and twin electric fuel pumps; the 3-liter (183-cubic-inch) inline six for the production versions would get their gas through direct mechanical injection, making the 300 SL the first "production" automobile to use fuel injection. This was another area in which Mercedes excelled. Daimler-Benz and Bosch had pioneered direct fuel injection in the 1930s for use on aircraft engines. They had also experimented with a fuel-injected, 4.5-liter V12 racing engine in 1939 and at one point had even considered using fuel injection for the 1952 300 SL competition cars.

*When automotive journalists first saw the 300 SL with its doors raised, someone commented that it looked like a seagull. Shortly thereafter they were commonly referred to as "gullwing" coupes.*

When the Bosch fuel-injection system finally appeared on the production coupes, it had been so well developed that its practicality and advantages were beyond dispute, but the 300 SL carried an auxiliary electric fuel pump at the tank to help overcome vapor lock in the injection pump and to provide a low-fuel reserve. The fuel-injected *Einspritzmotor* became standard Mercedes-Benz fare by the late 1950s, and Bosch fuel injection a performance car standard the world over.

An output of 215 horsepower was delivered via a 4-speed synchromesh gearbox and a ZF limited-slip differential. At peak performance the cars could attain a top speed of about 150 mph and clock zero to 60 in eight seconds, making the 300 SL the fastest production automobile available to the public at the time.

*The 3-liter, inline six-cylinder engine's 215-horsepower output arrived at the rear wheels via a 4-speed synchromesh gearbox and a ZF limited-slip differential. At peak performance the production 300 SL could attain 150 mph and reach 60 mph from rest in eight seconds. This was the fastest production sports car you could buy in 1954. The Daimler-Benz M 198 six-cylinder engine displaced 2,996 cubic centimeters with a bore x stroke of 85 x 88 mm.*

## MAKING A RACECAR CIVILIZED

Stylists Karl Wilfert and Paul Braiq transformed a racecar into a civilized—well, almost civilized—road-going sports car in less than a year. But beneath the streamlined bodywork, chrome trim, and luxuriously appointed interior, little else changed. Like a racecar driver, an SL owner and passenger had to clamber over the wide elbow-high doorsill to get in or out of the car, luggage was restricted to what could be packed behind the seats or in the optional leather suitcase, and in general, unless one had the driving skills of Stirling Moss, a 300 SL was a handful to manage.

The F.I.A. accepted the 300 SL in the Grand Turismo Class for international sports car racing even though it was a production road car. The presence of privately owned Gullwings at racing venues in the United States and throughout Europe in 1955 and 1956 brought as many accolades to Mercedes as the factory's racing efforts in 1952. And to covertly further the presence of their cars in the winner's circle, Mercedes-Benz produced 29 all-aluminum-bodied 300 SL competition cars for 1955 and 1956. The production cars were victorious in the 1955 Mille Miglia, Liège-Rome-Liège, Alpine, and Tulip rallies. The next year, a 300 SL finished 6th in the rain-soaked Mille Miglia, another took the checkered flags at the Acropolis and Sestrière rallies, Willy Mairesse won the Liège-Rome-Liège contest, and Stirling Moss finished second in the Tour de France. As a production road car the 300 SL made a great racecar.

Interestingly, just as importer Max Hoffman had predicted, roughly 1,000 cars, the majority of production between 1954 and 1956, were delivered to customers in the United States. Today these sporty two-seaters are among the most coveted of all post-war sports cars and a driving experience not to be missed. ◆

*When interior color and leather upholstery was not specified, this was the standard 300 SL color scheme, silver with blue plaid. Restored cars with blue plaid upholstery are rarely seen.*

# *No.* 23

## Alfa Romeo B.A.T. 5

### *Aerodynamics Italian-Style*

**ONE CAN ONLY IMAGINE THE BEWILDERMENT** of Italian motorists cruising along the *autostrada* in 1953 when the Bertone-bodied B.A.T. suddenly appeared in their rearview mirror. With its pincer-like front end, shallow roofline, and tall, curving rear fenders, it resembled a giant steel batfish mounted on wheels. Within the car's narrow cockpit the test driver pressed hard to wring every mile per hour out of the little four-cylinder, 90-horsepower engine . . . 110 mph, 115 mph, 120 mph, 122 mph, 123 mph . . . flat out and faster than any Alfa Romeo 1900 Sprint had ever gone. *Meraviglioso! Meraviglioso!* shouted the driver to the chase car, his left thumb raised to indicate a successful test run.

Outside of the Carrozzeria Bertone studio in Turin no one had ever seen a car that looked like this. Bertone's road tests on the Italian *autostrada* were becoming increasingly necessary to determine if the aerodynamic contours of the body were effective. This was before wind tunnels and computer-aided design models. Stylists worked on intuition, and the best way to test a design was to tape wool strings all over the body, run the car at high speed, and have a chase vehicle full of engineers watching to see how the wind affected the strings. If they blew straight back the air was flowing smoothly over the body. If they waved around erratically the wind was buffeting over the body. "This was very primitive but it worked well enough," Nuccio Bertone told the author in 1989.

*This high rear elevation exhibits the use of front fender air extractors to cool the brakes. The prominent inward curve of the tailfins and the tapered roofline acted as a central stabilizing element and the large, flush glass backlight directed airflow over the body to reduce wind resistance. Tests revealed that B.A.T. 5 had 38 percent less wind drag than a conventional 1900 Alfa Romeo.*

There were three experimental Alfas built, B.A.T. 5, followed by B.A.T. 7, and then B.A.T. 9, each a different variation, a refinement of aerodynamics and styling which led to the design of the 1955 Alfa Romeo Giulietta Sprint, one of the most successful cars in Alfa Romeo's history. More than 40,000 were built over 10 years.

B.A.T. was the acronym for Berlinetta Aerodinamica Tecnica, a design penned by one of Italy's most eccentric and talented automotive stylists, Franco Scaglione. The wiry, temperamental, chain-smoking designer had come to Bertone in 1951 after a brief tenure at Carrozzeria Pinin Farina. Scaglione was inspired by aircraft design and had caused quite a sensation at the 1952 Paris salon with his innovative Fiat-Abarth 1500 Coupe.

*The B.A.T. 5 interior was simple but elegant as only the Italian carrozzeria could do. Leather bucket seats, standard Alfa Romeo instruments, and a beautiful Nardi wood-trimmed steering wheel were all the accents necessary.*

The car had a trisected front end with twin air intakes and a central headlight flanked by a single headlight in each of the extended fender pods. The roofline was light with a large glass area and steeply inclined window, the rear reinforced by a slim central pillar. The wheel arches were scalloped to allow emissions of brake heat, and the elegantly rounded tail was surmounted by fins. This was the origin of the Alfa B.A.T. designs, what Scaglione described as "dynamics fluido." The concept of fluid dynamics was 20 years old by the 1950s, having been pioneered by German aerodynamicist Professor Wunibald Kamm, director of the Research Institute for Motoring and Vehicle Engines. Kamm had worked with Daimler-Benz on the Type 80 land speed record car in the 1930s. Scaglione studied Kamm's work and the works of Andreau, Everling, and Jayray, all of whom had theorized and experimented with aerodynamics. With the B.A.T. Scaglione turned theory in substance.

The number 5 car had four predecessors which never left the drafting table; B.A.T. 5 was constructed on the 90-horsepower, 1,975-cubic-centimeter Alfa Romeo Sprint platform and was first shown at the Turin Salon in 1953. Reaction from the world's automotive designers and stylists ranged from wonderment to abhorrence. Some years later when Scaglione was asked about the initial reaction to B.A.T. 5, he replied, "It is not without an element of presumption that such a car comes into being. One could call it a vague flavor of prophesy. But if we have done this, which in fact proposes different solutions to almost everything that is normal in car design and construction today, it is done with-

WALKING UP TO THE ALFA ROMEO B.A.T. IS LIKE APPROACHING SOMETHING FOREIGN, NOT ONLY IN NAME BUT IN ITS VERY PRESENCE. THIS IS ALL ABOUT STYLE AND WHAT IT CAN DO TO MAKE A CAR GO FASTER. SLIP BEHIND THE WHEEL AND YOU ARE SITTING IN A PRODUCTION ALFA STREET CAR, BUT OUTSIDE, THE AERODYNAMIC BODY IS ABOUT TO GIVE THIS PEDESTRIAN VEHICLE NEW-FOUND POWER. AT HIGHWAY SPEEDS, THE B.A.T. SLIPS THROUGH THE AIR AND YOU FEEL MORE LIKE YOU ARE SOARING THAN DRIVING A MERE 90-HORSEPOWER, ALFA ROMEO SPRINT.

out any intention of criticizing anybody." An answer almost as enigmatic as the car!

B.A.T. 7, built in 1954, and B.A.T. 9, completed in 1955, however outrageous in appearance, were evolutionary designs that pioneered practical aerodynamics for production sports and racing cars at a time when technology and innovation manifested themselves in the tip of a drafting pencil and the minds of stylists like Franco Scaglione. Driving an Alfa Romeo B.A.T. is driving history. ◆

*All of Scaglione's concepts with the B.A.T. were working, practical designs, however different they may have been from his contemporaries. Designing a car that could reach nearly 125 mph with a modest 90-horsepower engine and a simple Alfa Romeo 1900 suspension and skinny tires meant that the body had to cheat the wind. This was achieved in part by almost fully enclosing the front and rear wheels.*

# *No.* 24

## 1937 Cord 812 SC

### *Last Chance Classic*

**ASIDE FROM WILLIAM C. DURANT,** Errett Lobban Cord was perhaps the most colorful figure in the early history of America's thriving automotive industry. In addition to his expanding aviation businesses (later to become American Airlines), E. L. Cord had taken over The Auburn Automobile Co. in Auburn, Indiana; the Lycoming engine company; purchased a controlling interest in Duesenberg; bought the Limousine Body Company of Kalamazoo, Michigan, the Connersville and Central Manufacturing body companies in Indiana; and introduced America's first front-wheel-drive automobile. And he had done this all before 1930. Cord was in the enviable position of controlling virtually every company involved in the manufacturing and supplying of components for his automobiles. He was, in effect, a miniature General Motors. Unfortunately, in order to survive the economic depravities of the 1930s, Cord needed to be General Motors. By 1936, when the all-new 810 Cord was introduced, the Cord Corporation was nearing the end of a lost horizon.

The 810 and 1937 812 models have been hailed as the most beautiful automobiles ever designed, and while not everyone will agree with that, no one will question that they simply shocked the automotive industry out of its Depression-born complacency. In one bold stroke from his pen, stylist Gordon Buehrig brought a dramatic end to the way automotive designers looked at the front of an automobile. Buehrig had not only broken the traditional rules of design, he had rewritten them.

*The Cord 812 SC Sportsman was an elegant two-seater with remarkably graceful lines and unlike any other American car of the 1930s. The handsome pontoon fenders and sleek hood lines gave the car a sense of fluid motion even when standing still. The absence of a traditional grille shell and radiator mascot was unique for the 1930s. The hide-away headlights were concealed inside the fenders.*

*The SC was the sportiest of the 810 and 812 models.*

## THE ARTISTRY OF DESIGN

Gordon Miller Buehrig joined E.L. Cord's automotive empire in June 1929, and was only 25 years old when he was appointed chief body designer for Duesenberg. From his drafting table came some of the most celebrated automotive designs of the era, but from his position he could also see the writing on the wall, and in 1933 he resigned from Duesenberg, returning to the General Motors Art & Colour Department where he had started his career under Harley Earl in the late 1920s. Within a year, however, Duesenberg President Harold T. Ames had persuaded Gordon to return to Indiana and head up the design of an entirely new automobile. He was offered a chance to bend the rules—break the darn things clean off if he wanted to—just so long as he came up with a design no one had ever seen. It was a temptation someone of Buehrig's inestimable talent could not resist. He presented his design to Ames in the spring of 1934, and it was approved as a lower-priced companion model to the Model J Duesenberg, what LaSalle was to Cadillac.

As the Depression deepened, Buehrig was reassigned to Auburn to restyle the model line, which resulted in his creating the most famous Auburn model ever, the supercharged 851 Boattail Speedster. By the time he returned to Duesenberg headquarters in Indianapolis, his Baby Duesenberg design been appropriated by the Cord division, which wanted it as a successor to the discontinued L-29. Thus, the new Duesenberg became the basis for the 1936 Cord.

Buehrig had to redo the front end to accommodate the car's front-wheel-drive design, which essentially had the driveline reversed with the differential in front. Working in around-the-clock shifts, Cord managed to produce the 100 production cars required in order to display a new model at the 1935 New York Auto Show. They were completed by the eleventh

*A Bendix pre-selector vacuum shift transmission gave the Cord another unique feature. To select gears, the driver simply moved the small ring through the gated pattern of the miniature gearbox mounted to the right of the steering column and then released the clutch.*

hour, except that none of the cars were running! Based solely on Buehrig's styling, the Cord 810 was the hit of the New York show. Fortunately no one had asked for a test drive!

After the show, Cord set about the task of completing the cars and getting them into the hands of anxiously waiting owners.

For those who were willing to be patient, what awaited them was the most advanced automobile of 1936. The 810 was literally years ahead of anything else on the road.

## BREAKING NEW GROUND

So completely different from any other car of its time, the 810 was the first American automobile to have hidden door hinges, the first to introduce a one-piece, rear-hinged hood, concealed headlights, and the very first water-cooled automobile ever to abandon the use of a traditional front grille and radiator shell. Buehrig had indeed broken all of the rules.

Beneath the aerodynamic coachwork was an equally advanced driveline and chassis. Gordon's counterpart in engineering was Herbert C. Snow, the inventive designer who had pioneered the X-braced frame in American automobiles.

The state of the engineer's art had advanced considerably since Cord's first front-wheel-drive car. The new 810 design placed the specially-built 125-horsepower Lycoming eight-cylinder engine immediately aft of the front axle with the differential attached directly to the clutch housing. The new arrangement, coupled to a Bendix pre-selector vacuum shift transmission, gave the car a near perfect 55/45 front-to-rear weight ratio. The Bendix did away with the conventional floor-mounted shifter. To select gears, the

**SLIDING BEHIND THE WHEEL OF A CORD 810 OR 812 IS EXPERIENCING SOMETHING THAT WAS ALL NEW TO AMERICANS. YOU FACE A HANDSOME, ENGINE-TURNED DASHBOARD AND A MINIATURE GEARBOX EXTENDING FROM THE STEERING COLUMN. SLIDE THE LITTLE SHIFT LEVER, TAP THE CLUTCH AND YOU CHANGE GEARS. UNLESS YOU'VE DRIVEN A FRENCH CAR WITH A COTAL, THIS IS AN ENTIRELY NEW DRIVING SENSATION. UNFORTUNATELY, IT WASN'T ENOUGH OF A SENSATION TO SAVE CORD IN THE DEPTHS OF THE DEPRESSION.**

driver simply moved a small ring through a miniature gated gearbox mounted on a stalk at the right of the steering column and then released the clutch. The idea was based on the French Cotal pre-selector gearbox used on Bugattis, Delages, and Delahayes, and gave the Cord another unique feature to attract American buyers.

The 810 and 812 (the latter introduced in 1937 with an optional supercharged engine) were exceptionally well-balanced cars with a lower center of gravity than most and a lower unsprung weight. The powerful Lycoming engine, either normally aspirated or supercharged, delivered quick response—zero to 60 in 20 seconds—and with the blower, a mere 14 seconds elapsed before reaching the mile-a-minute mark. Equipped with Lockheed hydraulic brakes to bring the high-performance Cord down from speed with ease and reliability, basically everything on the car was done right; it was just done too late. For E. L. Cord's faltering automotive empire, it wasn't enough to turn the tide. On August 4, 1937, Cord decided to get out of the automobile business and concentrate on aviation. ◆

*The Cord 810 and 812 rank among the most beautifully styled cars of all time.*

Pro legibus ac regibus
1936
V-16 CADILLAC
Aero-Dynamic Coupe

# *No.* 25

## 1934 Cadillac V16 Aero-Dynamic Coupe

### *The Shape of Things to Come*

**IN THE 1930S, STREAMLINING WAS LIKE** a magical language that defied cultural, social, and economic differences. During this era of aerodynamic enlightenment, from the late 1920s up until the beginning of World War II, there were several schools of thought on the application of aerodynamic principles. Most were developed in France, Germany, and the United States. Interestingly, the concepts, even those adopted in Europe, had their roots in America through the work of visionaries Buckminster Fuller and Norman Bel Geddes. The theories of Fuller were elemental: To achieve greater speed, one needed to reduce, or eliminate, a vehicle's resistance to the wind. One way was to bludgeon it with sheer horsepower; the other was to slide through it like a rapier. Observed Bel Geddes, "Speed is the cry of our era, and greater speed is one of the goals of tomorrow."

That need for speed led to a convergence of styling, which appeared almost simultaneously in the 1930s at European Motor Shows and, in the United States, at the Chicago World's Fair Century of Progress Exposition in 1933, where Cadillac unveiled its streamlined V16 Aero-Dynamic Coupe. Bodied by Fleetwood and built on a Series 452-C chassis, the immense sixteen-cylinder car featured pontoon-type fenders and a streamlined, fastback roofline—a look that would not only influence GM automotive designs into the 1940s, but automotive styling the world over.

Streamlining was still in its developmental stages. Automakers had learned how to flow fender and rooflines and reduce the aerodynamic drag caused by such

*When GM's styling chief Harley Earl got wind of the forthcoming aerodynamic Pierce-Arrow Silver Arrow, planned to debut at the 1933 Chicago Century of Progress Exposition, GM's luxury car division and Fleetwood teamed up to design and build the 1933 Cadillac V16 Aero-Dynamic Coupe. In 1934, GM added the new body style to its custom catalog.*

*Attractive gold-faced instrumentation and a stylish banjo steering wheel accent the Cadillac V16 Aero-Dynamic Coupe interior.*

traditional styling cues as running boards, trunks, open fenders, and high, vertical rooflines. But having achieved progress in these areas, particularly with the Cadillac Aero-Dynamic Coupe, most designers had yet to address the wind resistance generated by upright radiators and grille shells, which was about the same as putting a 4' x 8' sheet of plywood in front of the car. It would take another generation before aerodynamics got around to the front of production cars.

In 1934 Cadillac began offering the Aero-Dynamic Coupe as a special order coachbuilt body for its V8, V12, and V16 chassis. The production models, such as this 1936 V16, were almost identical to the 1933 show car. Fleetwood produced a total of 20 Aero-Dynamic Coupes between 1934 and 1937, eight of which were for the V16 chassis. The car pictured was the nineteenth body built in the series, the next from the last V16. All of the production V16 models were mounted on Cadillac's immense 154-inch (12.8-foot) wheelbase chassis—the longest ever used on a Cadillac production car—and sold for $8,100. The 1933 Century of Progress show car had been built atop the 149-inch wheelbase chassis used that year for sixteen-cylinder models. Despite their size (nearly 18 feet from bumper-to-bumper) the cars

*Opposite. The fastback roofline introduced in 1933 would become a Cadillac styling trend by the start of World War II and would be picked up again in early postwar designs. More importantly, the fastback concept would become a design paradigm for automakers the world over.*

were easy to drive, with light steering and plenty of performance from the 165-horsepower, 452-cubic-inch V16 engine.

As well as being the most aerodynamic American car of the early 1930s, the Cadillac V16 was also one of the most advanced mechanically. Not only was this the first production V16 engine in America, it was the first to use hydraulic valve lifters. The V16 ran almost silently and was capable of delivering an Aero-Dynamic Coupe to a top speed of 100 mph. ◆

DRIVING A V16 CADILLAC IS NOT UNLIKE WHEELING AROUND IN A TRUCK. IT IS AN IMMENSE CAR, AND THOUGH IT STEERS WELL, IT NEEDS A LOT OF MANEUVERING ROOM. THE ENGINE, ONCE STARTED, IS WHISPER QUIET AND AT A STOP YOU BARELY KNOW IT IS RUNNING. THIS IS DRIVING AT ITS TECHNOLOGICAL BEST. SURROUND IT WITH THE AERO-DYNAMIC COUPE BODY AND YOU ARE ON THE CUTTING EDGE OF MOTORING FOR THE 1930S.

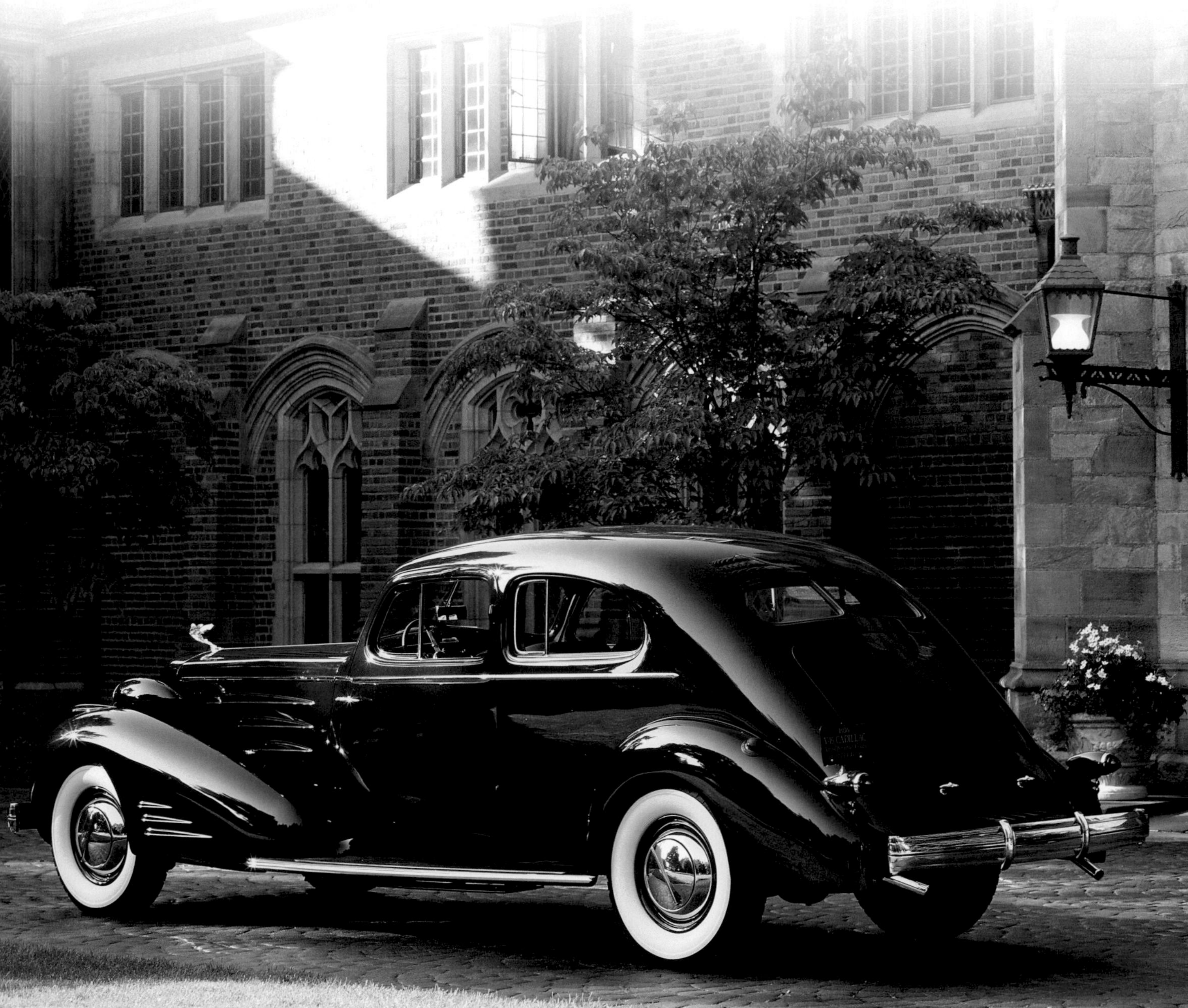

# No. 26

## FERRARI 275 GTB/4

### The Best Ferrari Road Car Ever

**DRIVING ANY FERRARI, PAST OR PRESENT,** is memorable, but there are a handful that can be best described as extraordinary. The 275 GTB/4 is at the top of that list. It was originally introduced as a twin-cam model in 1964, the first of Ferrari's now legendary 1960s Berlinettas available in either touring or racing configurations. Customers had the option of three Weber carburetors (with which the GTB was homologated for racing) or a phalanx of six Weber 40 DCN/3 carburetors, the more desirable and visually enticing of the two. There was even a choice of construction: a combination of steel and aluminum or an all-alloy competition body. Stylish Campagnolo 14-inch cast alloy wheels, re-creating the design used on the 1963 Typo 156 Formula One cars, were standard, with more traditional Borrani wire wheels as an option.

In his 1981 book, *Illustrated Ferrari Buyer's Guide,* noted Ferrari historian Dean Batchelor wrote: "The 275 series marked the progressive change in Ferrari design philosophy from thinly disguised racers to comfortable and luxurious transportation vehicles. Because of the chassis changes—primarily the four-wheel independent suspension—the 275s were not only faster, but more comfortable than their predecessors."

Equipped with the Colombo-designed 60-degree V12 displacing 3,286 cubic centimeters (77mm x 58.8mm bore and stroke) and dispensing 280 horsepower at 7,600 rpm with the triple Webers, the 275 GTB was the ultimate expression of Ferrari's ideology: a road car suitable for racing, that gave up little, if anything, to purebred competition models. With the latter in mind, Ferrari also produced a limited number of

*The shape was new, dramatic, and evocative of the triumphant 250 GTO racecars. The 275 GTB and GTB/4 were the most exciting sports cars Ferrari had ever offered at the time. (Bruce Meyer collection)*

*The Colombo-designed four-cam V12 had double overhead cams, dry sump lubrication, and six twin throat Weber carburetors. It rewarded owners with an exhilarating 300-horsepower output.*

275 GTB/C (C for *Competizione*) stripped down for out-and-out racing and equipped with a dry sumped engine and lighter weight bodywork.

Exactly two years after introducing the 275 GTB, Ferrari raised the stakes and brought out a new four-cam version at the Paris Auto Show. Jaguar had been building dual overhead cam (four-cam) engines since the late 1940s. Over the same period, Ferrari had been content to offer his single overhead cam V12 engines. By the early 1960s, more European road cars were appearing with four-cam engines, not only Jaguar, but some of Ferrari's toughest competitors: Aston Martin, Alfa Romeo, and Maserati, not to mention the new kid on the block, Lamborghini. Enzo Ferrari had little choice but to follow suit, but if he was going to join in, it would be on his terms, and as with most things Ferrari, the result was extraordinary.

The 275 GTB four-cam was derived from the 3.3- and 4-liter engines which had powered the 275 and 330 P2 prototypes of the 1965 racing season, engines which were descended from Colombo designs dating back to 1957. While the design was old, it was proven, and over a period of 17 years Ferrari increased his reliable 60-degree V12 more than 140 percent in horsepower. With the four-cam, Ferrari put a true competition-oriented road car into the hand of his admiring public, a car with double overhead cams, dry sump lubrication, six twin throat Weber carburetors, and a chest swelling 300 horsepower.

The freshened body design penned by Sergio

*Opposite. The rear quarters and backlight were very similar to those of the Scaglietti-designed, Le Mans-winning 250 GTO. By the time of the 275 GTB/4's introduction, the GTO was regarded as the greatest sports racing car in the world. The GTB and GTB/4 gave drivers a taste of that greatness.*

**HERE IS A CAR THAT DELIGHTS NOT ONLY THE EYES BUT THE BODY. ONE OF THE MOST BEAUTIFUL SPORTS CARS EVER DESIGNED, THE 275 GTB/4 IS ALSO ONE OF THE FASTEST OF ITS DAY, AND EVEN TODAY, FEW NEW SPORTS CARS ARE ITS EQUAL. THE INTERIOR IS ALL BUSINESS, BLACK AND UNADORNED, A RACECAR IN STREET CAR TRIM. LIGHT THE ENGINE AND THE COCKPIT FILLS WITH THE SOUND OF THE V12, SHIFT INTO GEAR, AND THE 275 GTB/4 WILL TAKE YOU BACK TO A TIME WHEN THE LINE THAT SEPARATED RACECARS AND ROAD CARS WAS ALMOST INVISIBLE.**

Pininfarina captured the best styling cues of the competition 250 GTO as well as the luxurious GTB Lusso. The 275 GTB and GTB/4 were the most aggressively styled road cars ever, with long plunging hoods, small oval radiator intakes, covered headlights, a pronounced hood bulge, short rear overhang, and fastback roofline, all perfectly harmonized to the contour of the steeply inclined windshield. Author Stanley Nowak wrote of the 275 GTB/4: "Like all of the best Ferraris, driving (the GTB/4) automatically focused one's concentration on getting the most out of it. It responded in kind. The more one puts into it, the more one gets out of it. Like most Ferraris, it is intended for serious drivers." If the car had any detractors, their only protest was that it too closely resembled the 250 GTO, something everyone was willing to live with! Even World Driving Champion Phil Hill (Ferrari 1961) described the 275 GTB/4 as a thinly disguised "boulevard version of the GTO."

While there are Ferrari enthusiasts who will argue the point, the majority will agree that the 275 GTB/4 is the best looking Berlinetta ever built. Of the four-cam models, only about 280 examples left the factory. This is one driving experience not to be missed. ◆

Pro legibus ac regibus

# *No.* 27

## 1967 Bizzarrini GT Strada 5300

### *Italian Style, America Guile*

"THE FIRST VISUAL IMPRESSION OF THE CAR IS ALMOST STARTLING. IT'S LONG, ULTRA LOW AND LOOKS LIKE IT IS DOING AT LEAST 100, SITTING STILL."

— *ROAD & TRACK*, NOVEMBER 1966

**THINK OF IT AS AN ITALIAN CORVETTE,** because the Bizzarrini GT Strada 5300 was exactly that. Back in the 1960s, independent Italian automakers were not calling Enzo Ferrari, Alfa Romeo, or Fiat asking to buy engines, they were on transatlantic calls dialing up General Motors, which was all too happy to sell Corvette V8 engines, transmissions, and driveline components to the Italians. To automakers like Giotto Bizzarrini, the best all-around engine that lire could buy was a 327-cubic-inch, 350-horsepower Chevrolet V8.

Bizzarrini is one of the most renowned of Italy's cottage industry sports and racecar builders, an offshoot as it were of Iso, another legendary Italian marque and the basis of the Bizzarrini Strada. A former Ferrari engineer, he left the company in 1961, a time when several of Enzo's designers and engineers made an exodus from Maranello to branch out on their own. Bizzarrini established a design and consulting firm in Livorno and his first major client was soon to be Ferrari's staunchest

*The Bizzarrini grand touring Berlinetta Tipo Strada 5300 had all the right design elements, sweptback body lines, a wide stance, and high wheel arches filled with tires.* Road & Track *said, "The Bizzarrini's handling borders on the fantastic for a road car." (Ron Spindler collection)*

*Not taking a page from Enzo Ferrari, Bizzarrini made his handful of sports cars as luxurious as possible. A lot of supple, hand-sewn leather for a two-passenger sports car.*

competitor, Ferruccio Lamborghini. Bizzarrini then began working for a wealthy industrialist named Renzo Rivolta, a former (and highly successful) refrigerator manufacturer who longed to be an automaker. Rivolta began by building mopeds, and in 1953, a little air-cooled 236-cubic-centimeter minicar named the Isetta. BMW took on the Isetta and put a 250-cubic-centimeter single-cylinder engine in it and a lot of lire in Rivolta's bank account for the licensing rights and manufacturing. With more money than Croesus, Rivolta's Iso SpA in Bresso, Milan, began developing a sports car, the Iso-Rivolta, to be powered by a Corvette V8. He turned to Carrozzeria Bertone for the body design, and, in 1963, to Giotta Bizzarrini for engineering, the result of which was the spectacular Iso Grifo A3C GT.

As much a sportsman as designer, Bizzarrini liked to race what he built. In 1964, he took a lightweight version of the Grifo to Le Mans and handily won the GT Class. With a win and plenty of money, he too decided to become an automaker and, following Rivolta's lead, turned to GM for engines. Bizzarrini's idea of a sports car was quite different from everyone else's in Italy, or the rest of the world for that matter. The fluid lines of the GT Strada 5300 measured a mere 43 inches at the roofline. The sleek, streamlined aluminum body was manufactured by BBM in Modena, and in the opinion of countless sports car enthusiasts, ranks as one of the most beautiful cars ever created —certainly one of the most aggressive looking. It was, however, very short-lived. Production lasted from 1965 to 1969, when Bizzarrini found he could no longer remain competitive against Rivolta and other better financed constructors such as Alejandro DeTomaso, Ferrucio Lamborghini, and Carroll Shelby, all of whom, with the exception of Shelby, were building cars he had helped design!

This rare Strada 5300 from the Ron Spindler collection is equipped with the original 365-horsepower, 327-cubic-inch Corvette V8 and an all-

SURROUNDED BY LUXURIOUS ITALIAN LEATHER, A DRIVER CAN ALMOST FORGET WHAT THIS CAR WAS DESIGNED TO DO. UNDER THE HOOD THE CORVETTE ENGINE BEGS TO BE LET LOOSE. BACK IN THE 1960S *ROAD & TRACK* TEST DRIVERS MANAGED TO GET A TOP SPEED OF 170 MPH OUT OF A STRADA 5300. INSIDE, THE LOW ROOFLINE AND WIDE STANCE MAKE YOU FEEL AS THOUGH THE CAR IS WRAPPED AROUND YOU.

synchro Muncie 4-speed gearbox. This was the optional engine for the car. Standard was the 350-horsepower hydraulic lifter engine. For competition, the more powerful mechanical lifter V8 was supplied and fitted with an aluminum intake manifold of Bizzarrini's own design, four two-barrel 45 DOCE Weber carburetors, polished ports and combustion chambers, high-carbon connecting rods, special camshaft, and short exhaust system. According to Bizzarrini, the cars delivered an astonishing 420 horsepower! In the 1960s, one-horsepower-per-cubic-inch for a production car was regarded as high output, so Bizzarrini's rework of the 327 was nothing short of extraordinary.

Built on a 96½-inch wheelbase, the cars were equipped with Dunlop four-wheel hydraulic disc brakes, Campagnolo Electron wheels, and Dunlop tires—6.00-15 front and 7.00-15 rear.

It is estimated that between 80 and 90 Bizzarrini GT Strada 5300 Berlinettas were built. Few in the overall scheme of automaking, but in such instances as this, fewer is better. This is one of life's little pleasures that only a few will ever experience. ◆

*Low and lean, the Strada 5300 used large ducts at the rear to vent brake heat and contribute to the car's aerodynamic stability. A similar design was used on the Ferrari 250 GTO.*

# *No.* 28

## 1939 Talbot-Lago T150SS "Lago Special"

### *The Teardrop Coupe*

**THE MOST FAMOUS OF** Carrossier Figoni et Falaschi designs is the Talbot-Lago T150SS "Lago Special." Although no more than a dozen examples were built, and no two exactly the same, the avant-garde styling of the Talbot-Lago teardrop body simply stunned the automotive world in the late 1930s. The entire body was composed of ovals, from the fenders to the ovoid cockpit and rear-hinged doors.

The cars were built for Major Anthony Lago, co-inventor of the Wilson pre-selector transmission (a British version of the Cotal), who had used his own wealth to purchase the nearly bankrupt Talbot works in Suresnes, France. Automobiles Talbot and Société Anonyme Darracq was the French subsidiary of Sunbeam-Talbot-Darracq, an old British company that had lost sight of the French market as well as any interest in it by 1934 when Lago stepped in.

He named his new company Talbot-Lago and re-established it by building elegant, sporting cars that could also double as racecars. While the factory workers in the old Suresnes works might had shaken their heads wondering how they were going to survive building racecars, by 1937 Talbot-Lagos were in contention with Europe's best, finishing 1st, 2nd, 3rd, and 5th in the French Grand Prix at Le Mans. Talbots also won the Tourist Trophy, finishing 1-2, and popular French racecar driver Raymond Sommer brought Lago a 1st in both the Marseille and Tunis Grands Prix. By 1938 Talbot-Lago was among the top three contenders in French motor racing! Customer orders were flowing in for Talbots that could be raced, as well as for cars

*Joseph Figoni based his design for the Talbot-Lago Special on a series of progressive ovoid forms, from the greenhouse to the fenders. There wasn't a straight line on the car. (Peter Mullin collection)*

AERODYNAMICS WAS THE UNDERLYING THEME. WHEN YOU ALIGHT IN THE DRIVER'S SEAT OF A TALBOT-LAGO TEARDROP COUPE, THE SENSATION IS THAT OF BEING COCOONED AS THE INTERIOR SURROUNDS YOU. ON THE ROAD IT IS A STREAMLINED RACECAR THAT DEMANDS YOUR CONSTANT ATTENTION TO SPEED, GEARS, AND IN COMPETITION, KNOWING WHEN TO BREAK, DOWNSHIFT, AND WHEN TO MAKE THAT ALL-IMPORTANT GEAR CHANGE TO TAKE FULL ADVANTAGE OF THE SIX-CYLINDER ENGINE'S MODEST BUT UNENCUMBERED POWER.

built simply for impressing one's friends with what was now a nationally recognized marque swathed in trophies and accolades. That's how you save a company through racing.

The body for the T150SS is a beautiful deception, designed by the French master of aerodynamic styling, Joseph Figoni. As with most of Figoni's "teardrops," the visual center of the body was formed around the wheels and fenders, the latter independent pods that flowed seamlessly into the body to elongate what was a rather short 105-inch wheelbase. The teardrop fenders gave the impression of a longer body by placing the center of their mass *behind* the axles, rather than over them as in a conventional body design. The other

*The oval shaped passenger compartment and oval rear-hinged doors made for a high roofline and a surprising amount of interior room for so small a car. The driver was provided with an expansive, engine-turned (damascened) dash panel and full instrumention.*

*This rear view clearly shows the offset of the fender's centerline to the axle. This served to elongate the car despite its short wheelbase. The fastback design was coming into vogue both in Europe and America by the late 1930s.*

phenomenon of proportion the Figoni design solved was the low-hood high-cab relationship. The passenger compartment, which was a large oval, sat high with large oval doors and windows. The large two-piece windshield gave the driver a clear view over the high-crowned fenders and the car looked as if it were racing down the wind, even when sitting at rest.

Under the long stretch of hood was a hemispherical head, inline six-cylinder engine derived from the Talbot-Darracq 3-liter design Lago had inherited with the factory. Developing 160 horsepower with its new Lago-Becchia designed cylinder heads, it was coupled to Lago's patented 4-speed Wilson pre-selector gearbox, which had become a favorite of race drivers. Fuel was dispensed through a trio of Solex carburetors and at full cry a Talbot-Lago coupe could reach nearly 120 mph. For the 1930s, a speed approaching two-miles-per-minute was sufficiently exhilarating for anyone not wearing racing goggles.

As every Talbot was a potential racecar, Lago designed its underpinnings for competition, relying on the same suspension design he had used since the mid-1930s: The front suspension was connected to the chassis by a single upper arm and a multi-leafed transverse spring on the bottom, strengthened with a large trailing arm tied to the frame rail. The rear suspension was a typical solid axle with leaf springs. It was nothing exceptional and even a bit out of date but it worked, and Talbots won races and that was all that really mattered.

While the handling and ride may have been less poised than a Mercedes-Benz or an Alfa Romeo of the same era, very few sports cars built could rival a Talbot-Lago's styling. Besides, you couldn't drive that fast along the Champs Élysées anyway. ◆

# No. 29

## 1964 Porsche 904 Carrera GTS

### *Forget about the 911*

**EXOTIC WAS NOT A WORD OFTEN USED** to describe a Porsche prior to 1964, the year the small German sports car maker introduced a competition bred road car named the Carrera GTS, "Carrera" after the great Mexican road race Porsche had won in 1954 with the Type 550. Internally it was the Type 904, a design and styling breakthrough for Porsche that utilized a mixture of steel and fiberglass for the body. As unique as that combination might have been for the early 1960s, the 904's styling and design intent were even more so.

The car was designed by Ferdinand Porsche's grandson, Ferdinand Alexander Porsche III, or Butzi, a childhood nickname that stuck with him for life. Ferry Porsche's eldest son, Ferdinand Alexander, had found his calling in the design studio, learning at the side of his father and grandfather's chief stylist, Erwin Komenda. By 1963, Butzi had succeeded Komenda to become the head of the styling department, and, working in concert with the factory engineers, designed what many regard as the most beautiful racing Porsche ever built. This was done at the very same time Butzi was heading up the design of an all-new road car, the 901, later to become the legendary Porsche 911. Despite the longevity of the 911, Butzi regards the 904 Carrera GTS as his signature design.

## A RECORD BREAKING CAR IN RECORD TIME

The decision to build a new sports racing model came in 1963, and in order to compete the following season, it had to be ready by February 1964. Facing a seemingly

*The lightweight composite body contributed only 180 pounds to the 904. Porsche adopted the deeply curved windshield from the 1961 Type 718 racecar (a predecessor to the 904), and the car's single parallelogram-action wiper system.*

impossible timetable, Butzi took the 904 from a concept on paper to a completed prototype in an unprecedented six months! The very first car entered in competition appeared at Daytona in February 1964, driven by Augie Pabst and Chuck Cassell, and though it did not finish the race it left a lasting impression. More than four decades later the Carrera GTS still looks up-to-date alongside new Ferraris, Maseratis, and Lamborghinis! In the entire history of automotive design, all the cars worthy of such praise can be counted on one hand.

Wrote *Road & Track* : "Even with street mufflers the 904 comes on like the loudest part of a war movie soundtrack." *Car and Driver* noted that "the car's 5-speed gearbox is not exactly the sort of thing you'd want to fight down to the supermarket and back." Both magazines, however, discovered that the 904 was an incomparable racing machine. As a road car it was better suited for the racetrack unless one had a passion for speed and the discomforts of a purebred racer.

The basis of the 904's design was a pressed steel chassis on to which a lightweight glass fiber (fiberglass) body was bonded. Butzi recalled that the first use of plastics was to mold racecar seats to fit individual drivers. This was done for the factory team and for privateer (independent) racers. Previously, seats had been pounded out of sheet metal. Fiberglass was easier. "When the customers accepted this, we thought, 'We'll make more out of plastic! Why don't

*The overlap of the plastic upper to the steel underbody became a styling cue, a "run through" that defined the shape of the car by wrapping around the rear to form an integral spoiler. (Kent Rawson collection)*

we make a whole car?'"[1] As it turned out, they made half a car, from the beltline up.

Using fiberglass was nothing new. Chevrolet had used it to build the Corvette since 1953; Bill Devin had used plastic for his sports cars as had Dutch Darrin in the 1950s, but Porsche's application of glass fiber was unique because no one had ever combined it with a steel body. The overlap of the plastic upper to the steel underbody became a styling cue, a "run through" that defined the shape of the car by wrapping around the rear to form an integral spoiler. If you see more than a passing resemblance to the later Ferrari (Fiat) Dino, it is no coincidence. The Carrera GTS would influence a number of sports car designs throughout the 1960s and 1970s.

1. *Porsche Legends* by Randy Leffingwell, page 82.

*A trio of new Carrera GTs await delivery outside the Porsche factory in 1964. (Porsche AG photo/author's collection)*

## SELLING A NEW IDEA

Mounted in the rear of the 904 was Porsche's venerable four-cam, four-cylinder engine dispensing 180 brake horsepower through a 5-speed gearbox and ZF limited-slip differential. The cars were to be homologated into the Group 3 Grand Touring class, meaning that 100 examples had to be built. Once the 904 was unveiled, however, selling 100 presented little problem for Porsche. It was affordably priced and also quite suitable as a road car. One of the first went to Stirling Moss. Another was purchased by legendary American sportsman Briggs Cunningham and raced by him at Le Mans in 1964, winning the under 3-liter prototype class (as the cars had not yet been homologated) and finishing 9th overall. Another pair was

AS A ROAD CAR THE 904 WAS A HANDFUL. EVERYTHING ABOUT THIS PORSCHE FEELS CRUDE BUT REFINEMENTS FOR RACECARS WERE FUNCTIONAL, NOT COMFORTABLE. THE SOUND IS DEAFENING, THE HEAT INSIDE THE COCKPIT IS BEARABLE BUT "COMFORTABLE" WOULD NOT BE AN APT DESCRIPTION. ONCE UNDER WAY, HOWEVER, THE SHIFTER GLIDES THROUGH THE GEARBOX AS REVS INCREASE AND THE ROAD FLASHES BY. ONCE YOU FIND YOUR PLACE BEHIND THE WHEEL, YOU CAN UNDERSTAND THE SENSE OF SUPERIORITY RACERS FELT WHEN DRIVING A 904 CARRERA. IT HAS A WONDERFUL BALANCE UP TO THE LIMIT, BUT STEP OVER THE THRESHOLD AND ONE NEEDS THE SKILLS OF MOSS, PABST, OR CUNNINGHAM TO DRIVE IT WELL.

delivered to Los Angeles auto importer and race team owner Otto Zipper.

Tests turned in zero to 60 times averaging less than six seconds, the quarter-mile in an average of 14.3 seconds, and a top speed just shy of 160 mph.

*The basic wheel and brake assemblies were taken from the production Porsche 356C but used light alloy rims fitted with Dunlop 165x15 SP radial ply tires. Suspension was a four-wheel independent racing-type with parallel wishbones.*

Exhilarating figures for 1964, but at a cost. Wrote *Car and Driver*, " . . . when you lose it, you lose it faster than the reflexes can follow. Not that it can't be done; the corrections must be quick, sure, and metered out in exact amounts at the right time."

The design of the Carrera GTS allowed Porsche to utilize a variety of engines for competition: the four-cam four-cylinder delivering 155 horsepower for non-racing road cars and 180 horsepower at 7,200

*Porsche Carrera GTs finished 1-2 in the 1964 Targa Florio. (Porsche AG photo/author's collection)*

rpm for competition (the difference being the addition of a road-going exhaust system); the new horizontally opposed six-cylinder designed for the 911; and an eight-cylinder racing engine. The four-cam, four-cylinder version was the most popular.

In 1964 Porsche 904s won the Targa Florio. In 1965 they won the Spanish Rally, Hellbronner, Rossfiel, Nürburgring, and Gaisberg races. A year later, American Sam Posey won the Watkins Glen 500 driving a Carrera GTS.

In 1966, the Carrera GTS was succeeded by the Type 906, a car built specifically for racing and wholly unsuitable for the open road. The Carrera GTS was the last true road and racecar of its era. Porsche built approximately 110. ◆

# No. 30

## 1957 BMW 507

### The Gullwing's Rival

**THE BMW 507 SPORT ROADSTER** is one of those rare cars that became a success after first being a failure, a failure that came at BMW's own hands. The 507 arrived too late and even though it was in almost all respects a superior sports car, it was overshadowed in the late 1950s by an even greater sports car, the Mercedes-Benz 300 SL.

While Mercedes-Benz had nearly been destroyed by the war, the company was able to rebuild itself by the end of the 1940s. BMW, which was developing jet engines for the Luftwaffe, was no less devastated by the allied forces, which regarded the BMW factories as a significant target. When the war ended and Germany was divided into East and West, the BMW factories were on one side and management on the other. And the factories were on the wrong side. A full decade would pass before BMW would build another automobile.

### BMW'S POSTWAR RESURRECTION

By 1951, BMW was back in business and had introduced its first postwar model, the six-cylinder Type 501 sedan. In 1952, the company introduced a new 2.6-liter V8 along with an improved 502 series and two additional cars, a sporty two-door Cabriolet and two-door Coupe. The latter two were intended to compete directly with Mercedes-Benz and its new 220 series. The BMWs were attractively styled and in the opinion of many historians better looking cars than the new Mercedes. What BMW

*The 507 Sport Roadster was BMW's answer to the Mercedes-Benz 300 SL. Had the company been able to produce them in sufficient numbers, it is possible the BMW might have eclipsed the early success of the Mercedes. (Mike Tillson collection)*

*The revised V8 in the 507 used a high lift camshaft and high compression ratio to deliver an impressive 150 horsepower at 5,000 rpm.*

lacked was a sports car to rekindle the heritage of the legendary 328 sports racing models from the 1930s. Sales director Hanns Grewenig told management this was necessary more than a year before Mercedes-Benz introduced the 300 SL, an event that brought BMW's board of directors to their collective feet. In record breaking time the company developed the 507 Sport Roadster which was ready in prototype form for the 37th Frankfurt Motor Show in September 1955, a little over 18 months after the 300 SL's debut.

## TAKING ON MERCEDES-BENZ AND THE 300 SL

The body design was penned by Count Albrecht Graf Goertz, an associate of famed international designer Raymond Loewy. By November 1954 he had completed two design studies and BMW accepted both, resulting in the production of three new sports models, the 503 Coupe and companion Cabriolet, and the high performance 507.

At its Frankfurt debut the 507 Sport Roadster overshadowed the 300 SL, and had BMW actually been prepared to build the cars in 1955, they could have stolen all of Mercedes' thunder. In almost every respect the 507 was a superior sports car.

Built on a 97.6-inch wheelbase, the 507 used a bizarre but highly effective suspension design

THE SOUND OF THE ENGINE IS ROUSING, AND THE BMW 507'S EXHAUST NOTE COMES BOOMING FROM BEHIND YOUR HEAD AS THE WIND RUSHES OVER THE STEEPLY ANGLED WINDSHIELD. IN THE WORLD OF 1950S SPORTS CARS THE 507 WAS THE EQUAL OF MERCEDES AND FERRARI, SOMETHING THAT EVEN ONE STINT BEHIND THE WHEEL WILL CONFIRM.

employing a longitudinal torsion bar for each wheel—those for the front anchoring at the center crossmember and those for the rear at the front tube. The independent front suspension used conventional parallel wishbones, while the rear used a trailing wishbone above a solid axle, with the transverse lever arms placed below and on each side. This confusing arrangement nevertheless endowed the 503 and 507 models with excellent handling and cornering capabilities. Fitted with large 16-inch wheels, the 507 Sport Roadster had an impressive, wide stance. The passenger compartment was lean, narrowed at the

*From the front, the traditional BMW grille was stretched between the headlights.*

waist, and fitted with sporty cutaway doors. Goertz had designed a stunningly handsome sports car with a character and aggressive styling that would influence European—particularly Italian—sports car designers well into the 1960s.

Under the long stretch of hood was a revised V8 that delivered an impressive 150 horsepower at 5,000 rpm. Using a conventional floor-mounted 4-speed gearbox, the 507 was capable of 137 mph, making it one of the fastest cars on the market, second only to the 300 SL.

Compared to the cramped and claustrophobic Gullwing Mercedes, the BMW 507 was not only more graceful in appearance, it was a convertible. It was a joy to drive, less restrained by a race bred heritage, quick to respond, remarkably comfortable, and from every angle the very image of a pure sports car meant for the open road. And it should have been a rousing success. So where did things go wrong? New York importer Max Hoffman had envisioned selling several hundred 507 Sport Roadsters a year at a price of $5,000 each. However, production for 1956 was negligible and the following year BMW built fewer than 100 cars. Unlike Mercedes-Benz, which had an efficient assembly line for the 300 SL, BMW was manufacturing the aluminum-bodied 507s almost by hand. Making matters worse, labor costs were soaring and by the time the cars reached Hoffman's Manhattan dealership, the retail price had increased from $5,000 to $9,000. The final blow came in 1957 when Mercedes-Benz replaced the Gullwing Coupe with the new 300 SL Roadster. More plentiful and only slightly more expensive at $10,970, the Mercedes captured the hearts, minds, and wallets of Hoffman's clientele, who may have coveted a BMW 507 but chose not to wait. Sales being dependent on production, one has only to follow the money to find the answer to the Sport Roadster's demise. Hoffman couldn't sell what BMW couldn't deliver.

Over a period of four years BMW only managed to build 253 cars. Between 1956 and 1959 Mercedes-Benz had produced nearly 1,000 cars. The 300 SL Roadster remained in production through 1962 with total sales of 1,858 cars.

Had BMW been able to produce 500 Sport Roadsters a year, instead of fewer than 100, the most successful German sports car of the 1950s might have worn a blue and white roundel instead of a silver star. ◆

RRJ·704

# No. 31

## 1969 Dodge Charger Daytona

### *The Real Days of Thunder*

"WELL, THERE'S ONE OBVIOUS THING ABOUT A CHARGER DAYTONA. NOBODY, BUT NOBODY, WALKS BY WITHOUT BREAKING HIS NECK TO TAKE A SECOND LOOK."

— BOBBY ISAACS, 1970 NASCAR CHAMPION

**IN THE LATE 1960S THE FLEXING OF MUSCLES** could be heard from Detroit's Woodward Avenue to Van Nuys Boulevard in Southern California, as American automakers delivered into the hands of red-blooded males the most powerful street cars since the halcyon days of the 1930s supercharged SJ Duesenbergs. Not to say that a Dodge Daytona or its Plymouth Superbird counterpart were the modern day equivalent of a Duesenberg, but simply that American automakers hadn't installed so much power under the hood of a production street car in quite a few years. In Europe, homologation rules had unleashed hundreds of sports cars bred from racing stock, but in America this was uncommon.

Of the two winged wonders, the Dodge Daytona came first, rolling off the assembly line in 1969 with one goal in mind: a NASCAR championship for Dodge. This was achieved by Bobby Isaacs who, in addition to helping claim the NASCAR title for Dodge in 1970, set a closed-course speed record of 201.104 mph, a record

*The towering metal wing applied 600 pounds of downforce and increased the vehicle's stability at high speeds.*

*Little on the inside indicated you were behind the wheel of a championship racecar.*

that stood unbroken for 13 years! By the end of the 1970 season Dodge owned the NASCAR title.

Was this really a street car, you ask? Well, yes and no. It was a racecar built for the street, and as such production was limited to just enough to qualify the Daytona for NASCAR, a number totaling only 503 examples, nearly all of which had to be sold through Dodge dealers.

The cars were based on the 117-inch wheelbase 1969 Dodge Charger 500 shell fitted with a sloped, pointed nose jutting out 18 inches, and at the rear, a full width wing mounted on towering vertical struts. There was also an under-nose spoiler, vertical stabilizers, and a backlight modification. The nose and tail, along with reverse-mounted scoops over air-extracting holes cut into the fenders, were assembled and mounted at Creative Industries in Detroit, which was responsible for building the finished cars.

The Daytona had to be publicly introduced by April 15, 1969, in order to homologate for the September 1969 races. NASCAR boss Bill France had built a new super speedway near a small Alabama town called Talladega. It was higher banked and a little longer than the Daytona International Speedway and Dodge brass wanted the Daytona on that race track when it opened in September. After an arduous 10-month dash from paper to sheet metal, 503 Dodge Daytonas were built and ready for sale before the opening day at Talladega. NASCAR was so stunned by this that they sent a team to physically count the cars. Dodge was in the race. During practice at Talladega on September 9, driver "Chargin' Charlie" Glotzbach ran three laps in the developmental prototype (a nice way of saying test mule), his third lap blowing past the timing tower at an unprecedented 199.987 mph, faster than any car had ever clocked in NASCAR competition.

WHETHER THE ENGINE IS A HEMI OR A 440, THE POWER TO THE REAR WHEELS IS UNRELENTING. BURNING RUBBER WITH EVERY SHIFT IS ALMOST IMPOSSIBLE IF YOU'RE PUSHING THE REDLINE. STAND ON THE DAYTONA'S THROTTLE AND IT WILL STUFF YOU BACK IN THE DRIVER'S SEAT LIKE A SUCKER PUNCH.

The first Daytona sold, interestingly enough, was to the local sheriff, who took delivery of the black car and had it properly affixed with Sheriff's Department stars on the doors and a big rotating blue light mounted in the middle of the wing! He parked it at the entrance to Talladega on race day. Dodge couldn't have invented a better promotional stunt.

Although there were serious issues on opening day and many of the drivers, including Richard Petty, pulled out of the 500-mile race, Dodge came away with a victory thanks to driver Richard Brickhouse, who blistered around the track turning consecutive laps of 197 mph in the final minutes to finish seven seconds ahead of the 2nd place car. Dodge didn't win the NASCAR title in 1969, which went to Ford, but the following year with both the 1969 Daytonas and 1970 Superbirds racing, the NASCAR championship finally came home to the house of Chrysler.

The Daytona and Superbird are among the most unusual and desirable automobiles of the sixties and seventies, cars that will guarantee one of the most interesting experiences you'll ever have behind the wheel of an American muscle car. ◆

*The Daytona's pointed snout and chin spoiler worked as planned and provided 200 pounds of downforce as the car sliced through the wind.*

# *No.* 32

## 1967 Lamborghini Miura

### *Ferruccio's Raging Bull*

**THERE'S A STORY ABOUT THE REASON** Ferruccio Lamborghini started building sports cars. How true it is, no one really knows, but considering the two individuals involved and the nature of their disagreement, it could very well have gone something like this.

Lamborghini was a successful manufacturer of farming equipment, predominantly tractors, and he had built his business with the sweat and labor that accompanied Italy's post-World War II rebuilding. He started his business modifying surplus war vehicles into farm tractors and in 1952 finally began building his own line of sturdy, reliable tractors. At the same time Enzo Ferrari was beginning to manufacture road cars to complement his racing cars. A decade later successful Ferruccio bought one of successful Enzo's sports cars and found it less than satisfactory. Most would have lived with it but Lamborghini went to Maranello and told Ferrari what was wrong with the car. *Il Commendatore* did not receive this criticism well, and this being before the concept of good customer relations, told Mr. Lamborghini in so many words that if he thought he could build a better car he should do so. Such chastising from Ferrari would have turned most men into a pillar of salt, but instead, in 1963, the 47-year-old tractor builder began manufacturing sports cars.

The first Lamborghini was unveiled at the annual auto show in Turin, Italy, and was not particularly well received. A rough translation of one review described the body design as confused. It actually wasn't that bad, it just needed a little

*This early 1967 model was originally owned by singer and actor Dean Martin. It was purchased from him, with a blown engine, by a young stand-up comic who claimed to have some experience working on cars. His name was Jay Leno. The* Tonight Show *host still owns and drives the car today.*

improvement. Ferruccio took this in stride and turned the redesign of the 350 GTV over to Carrozzeria Touring, one of the most successful design houses in Europe. Touring was also coachbuilder to Ferrari!

The design staff reworked the front end and fenders of the 350 GTV into a sleek, sculptured body that even today can turn heads. The following March, Lamborghini was back at the Turin show with the 350 GT (having dropped the V and most of the original design with it), and this time the reviews were laced with superlatives.

## GOING FERRARI ONE BETTER

What Lamborghini had not found in need of changing was the 60-degree V12 engine beneath the hood, which had been designed by ex-Ferrari engineer Giotto Bizzarrini. For 1964 it was equipped with six horizontal Weber carburetors and delivered a rousing 270 horsepower at 7,000 rpm through a 5-speed, all-synchromesh gearbox manufactured in Germany by ZF. Wide open, the 350 GT could reach 150 mph. To Ferruccio's satisfaction, enthusiasts and critics regarded his new sports car, which bore the company's emblem displaying a bull at its center, as a more sophisticated design than a comparable 1964 Ferrari. The V12s from Maranello had two overhead camshafts; Lamborghini used four. He used six carburetors instead of three and a 5-speed gearbox instead of Ferrari's 4-speed with overdrive. In America, *Car and Driver* boasted, "It is much less demanding to drive than a Ferrari, and what is more, it seems to steer, stop, go and corner just about as well as our Ferrari test car (275 GTS), but it is so smooth, and so quiet."

## THE NAKED CHASSIS

Not one to rest on his laurels, Lamborghini set about building an even better sports car and in 1965 displayed a bare chassis at Turin named the P400 (for *Posteriore 4 litre*), shown sans coachwork to reveal its groundbreaking engineering. The new Lamborghini had a transverse rear-mounted engine.

Renowned Italian stylist Nuccio Bertone offered to design a body for the P400 and Lamborghini graciously accepted the offer. The following March the first Lamborghini P400 Miura was introduced at the Geneva Motor Show. The Bertone body, designed by stylist Marcello Gandini, was as unique as the car's mid-mounted engine, revealed by pivoting up the entire rear portion of the body, which separated just forward of the wheel arch. The shape was sensuous, as few cars have been, and the response overwhelming. Overwhelming because Lamborghini was not prepared to produce the Miura as quickly as the demand arose. In an effort to capture the momentum of its debut, the factory built the cars too quickly, and in turn they lacked some of the refinements expected by customers. These oversights were at best minor issues like the untinted windshield, which sloped so far back over the occupants that they baked in the brilliant Italian sunshine. The passenger compartment was small, ventilation modest, and no one had yet thought to offer air conditioning. And a radio wasn't even considered, as one would have been hard pressed to hear it over the roar of the V12 sitting only inches behind the driver and passenger. Nevertheless, the Miuras were glorious sports cars.

Early road testers were at a loss for adjectives to personify the Miura. They were also unable or unwilling to find the car's top end. In April 1970, *Road & Track*'s review of a Miura S indicated a top speed of 168 mph, 0 to 60 in a scant 5.5 seconds, 0 to 100 in 12.3 seconds, and the quarter mile in 13.9. Such performance came at a price. The Miura sold for $20,000, the equivalent of $114,000 today.

As Jay Leno notes, the Miura was one man's idea of what a sports car should be. It helps to be short, slim and Italian, and to have a love for the open road. The Miura is so low to the ground you feel like you're sitting on the road. The windshield so rakish it almost goes over your head and the sun pours into the interior. The Miura handles as lean as it looks.

After the initial rush was over, Lamborghini made all of the necessary improvements to the car to make it more civilized. Flaws were corrected, amenities such as power windows appeared, and the car achieved an enviable stature both in Italy and in the United States, where Lamborghini became as popular as Ferrari in the 1960s.

Says Leno, "It has a definite sense of style, one man's idea of what a sports car should look like as opposed to wind tunnel tests and all that, which is probably a better way to do it, but you just don't see many sports cars like the Miura that were styled with no outside influences." ◆

*The Bizzarrini-designed V12 in the Miura delivers a robust 350 horsepower, later increased to 370 horsepower in the Miura and 385 horsepower at 7,850 rpm in the Miura SV. Suspension was independent all around with double transverse wishbones.*

# No. 33

## 1935–36 Auburn Boattail Speedster

### The Most Beautiful American Car of the 1930s

**MOST WILL AGREE THAT THE** Auburn Boattail Speedster, if it is not *the* most beautiful American car built in the 1930s, certainly ranks in the top three. This was capturing lightning in a bottle, a robust sporting car with Hollywood silver screen character, a booming supercharged eight-cylinder engine, and an affordable Auburn Automobile Co. price tag.

The Auburn 851 and 852 (1935–1936) was the company's last great effort to survive the economic tidal wave that had washed prosperity from every corner of the nation by the mid-1930s. Auburn was one of America's oldest automakers and had formed the foundation for E. L. Cord's automotive empire in the late 1920s. With Auburn as the low-priced prestige leader, Cord as the mid-level model line, and Duesenberg as the luxury leader, E. L. Cord had created a small version of General Motors, right down to owning his own engine company, Lycoming, and several coachbuilders. He controlled every aspect of Auburn Cord Duesenberg design, engineering, and manufacturing, and was able to produce cars that offered exceptional value for the price, particularly Auburn.

*Success cannot always be measured in dollars and cents. In 1935–36 the Auburn 851/852 Boattail Speedster was a loss leader, a sporty two-seater intended to draw customers into Auburn showrooms, where they might purchase a less expensive Auburn model. More than 70 years later they are regarded among the most beautiful automobiles ever designed. Fortunately, stylist Gordon Miller Buehrig lived long enough to know that his designs survived the company.*

## CORD THE SAVIOR

The 1936 models were the end of the line, one that had its beginnings shortly after the turn of the last century, in 1903. The Indiana company was founded by Frank and Morris Eckhart and their first product was a single-cylinder runabout that sold for $800. Larger engines and more accommodating coachwork followed and by 1912, the company was doing well but the Eckharts never seemed to stay ahead of the wolf, and after World War I they were facing bankruptcy. Rather than folding their tents they took in a partner, William Wrigley Jr., and a consortium of Chicago investors. Despite the infusion of cash, the company still lacked an adequate dealer network and the postwar recession drove sales down to under 4,000 cars a year between 1919 and 1922. It was 1924 when Errett Lobban Cord arrived to take control of the company. Already a well known sales and marketing manager, the 30-year-old Cord assessed the company's situation, ordered changes in the cars, including redoing existing inventory, and sold off 750 cars on hand, enough to pay off the company's current debts. Cord was appointed vice president and two years later ascended to the presidency after becoming Auburn's chief stockholder. Under his tenure, Auburn prospered as never before with sales reaching 20,000 cars annually by 1929.

With cars powered by both six- and eight-cylinder engines, Auburn had quality, style, and with the Auburn straight eight engine, exhilarating performance.

*Opposite. The secret under the hood and behind the stylish flex pipe exhausts was a Lycoming-built straight eight coupled to a Schwitzer-Cummings supercharger. Every Auburn Speedster was a guaranteed 100 mph two-passenger sports car.*

*Below. With one of the snazziest dashboards of the 1930s, the Auburn Boattail Speedsters had everything going for them inside and out.*

*It was the most car and the most engine for the money in America. The Lycoming-built straight eight and Schwitzer-Cummings supercharger project, which was headed by Augie Duesenberg, placed one of the most powerful engines available in America under the hood of one of the most affordable cars of its time. The 280-cubic-inch engine delivered 150 horsepower.*

Despite the stock market crash in 1929, Auburn continued to sell cars at an astounding rate. The popularly priced Auburns soared to a sales record of 32,301 cars by 1931 as a result of Cord's dealer expansion program, plus an all-eight-cylinder line of cars at bargain prices.

When the nation's economic freefall finally caught up with Auburn, sales plunged to fewer than 8,000 cars in 1932 and a meager 4,703 the following year. Cord's response in 1932 was to introduce a new line of cars powered by a V12 engine and priced competitively with other eight-cylinder makes. The lowest priced Auburn V12 was under $1,000. As beautiful and as powerful as they were, the twelve-cylinder Auburns were the victim of their own perceived value. In the depths of the Depression few people wanted a V12 at any price.

## ONE LAST CHANCE

In an effort to save the company, which had invested half a million dollars to design the new 1934 models, Cord placed Duesenberg president Harold T. Ames in charge of Auburn with orders to turn things around. Ames brought his top designer, Gordon Buehrig, who had penned the greatest Duesenberg bodies of the era. With a modest $50,000 budget, Buehrig was charged with restyling the 1935 models in an effort to increase sales. He turned his attention to the front end sheet metal, grille, and fenders. The results were stunning. The flagship model was the

*Opposite. The Boattail body design was not Buehrig's alone. He refined the original concept for Duesenberg in the early 1930s and further developed it for the 1935–36 Auburns. Built on a short 127-inch wheelbase, the 851/852 models are among the sportiest American cars ever produced.*

**Slide into the driver's seat of this mechanical comet, with its massive front end, flowing fenders, and chromed exhausts and prepare to drive a legend. The passenger compartment seems incredibly small for such an immense automobile but this is little more than the cockpit of an Earthbound aircraft. Ignite the engine, slip the gearshift into place, and hold on. With the blower engaged this car is fast, loud, and unspeakably fun to drive.**

new 851 Speedster powered by a Lycoming straight eight engine coupled to a Schwitzer-Cummings supercharger. The cars also were equipped with a Columbia 2-speed rear axle allowing lower gearing for quicker acceleration, combined with a higher final drive ratio for improved top speed.

Each car was tested by legendary racer Ab Jenkins and certified to have reached a top test speed of 100.8 mph before being shipped. It was so stated on a metal dash plaque attached to every Auburn Speedster and signed by Jenkins, who became the first American to set a record 100-mph average for a 12-hour endurance run.

Even priced at a modest $2,245 (a 1935 Cadillac V8 Fleetwood Convertible Coupe, without a supercharger, sold for $4,045), Auburn could not generate enough sales to make a profit. Cord and Duesenberg were also bleeding red ink, and E. L. Cord was about to close the doors at all three companies and turn his full attention to the future of mass transportation, aviation.

The 1936 Auburn sedans, phaetons, and speedsters would be the last to bear the proud old Indiana name. At least with the 851 and 852 Boattail Speedsters, one of designer Gordon Buehrig's greatest achievements, the company went out in style. ◆

# *No.* 34

## 1915 PACKARD 5-48

### *The Packard Six, the Best Getaway Car of 1915*

**IT CAME TO BE KNOWN AS** "The Dominant Six" but around Packard everyone called the Model 5-48 "Jesse Vincent's Hot Rod." Jesse, the company's chief engineer, built a fast car. It wasn't intended to be a car known for its unsurpassed speed, but it turned out that way just the same. In a 1915 Packard advertisement, Jesse Vincent was quoted as saying, "Be careful how you step on this car. It leaps like a projectile."

In the first decade of the twentieth century, Packard was doing as well as any independent automaker in the country—better than most, actually. Packard was at the forefront of the American automotive industry by the mid-1910s. Following more than a decade of reliable four-cylinder models, the 5-48, or Packard Six, was added in 1912, a design originated by Packard's first chief engineer Russell Huff (who became a consulting engineer when Vincent assumed the top developmental position within the company), and completed by Vincent. Although the Six quickly became Packard's most popular model, the venerable four-cylinder cars, the Thirty and Eighteen, would remain in production for yet another year.

The Six, like the companion four-cylinder models, was offered in a wide variety of body styles, a total of 13, and a choice of three wheelbases, 139-inch, close-coupled 133-inch, and a short 121½-inch span for the Runabout body style. These were the most expensive Packard models produced, with prices ranging from $5,000

*The Packard Six was the largest car Packard built. In 1914 and 1915 the 4-48 and 5-48 Series were available on a 12-foot wheelbase (144 inches) with an overall length of 204½ inches. The popular Touring model sold for $4,850 in 1915.*

"IMMENSE" ONLY BEGINS TO DESCRIBE THE PACKARD 5-48. FOR A CAR OF SUCH GREAT MASS, FLOORING THE ACCELERATOR PEDAL SETS THE CAR INTO MOTION WITH A RUSH OF ENERGY. AT A MILE-A-MINUTE YOU REALIZE WHY BANK ROBBERS, WHO OFTEN HAD THE FINANCIAL WHEREWITHAL TO DRIVE THE BEST CARS, CHOSE TO LEAVE THE SCENE OF THE CRIME BEHIND THE WHEEL OF A PACKARD DOMINANT SIX!

to $6,550. For the price of a Packard Six one could have purchased a nice home in 1912!

The Packard Six had a massive engine with a swept volume of 525 cubic inches, (4½ in. x 5½ in. bore x stroke) and an output of 82 horsepower, giving the car what Packard called "The Fastest Getaway—60 Miles an Hour in 30 Seconds from a Standing Start." While that may not sound very impressive today, in 1915 it was a startling speed for anything not built for racing at Indianapolis. The last of the series, the 5-48 or Fifth 48, as it was also known, set a record at the Indiana Speedway, clocking 70 miles in just one hour. Packard noted this feat in its advertising, proclaiming the Dominant Six as "Boss of the Road."

The Packard's high-speed capability became so well known that by 1915 it was practically adopted as the official getaway car of the underworld, one that could easily outrun the lower-priced automobiles used by local and state law enforcement agencies. As early as 1913, *The Packard,* the automaker's official publica-

*The lengthy Packard chassis allowed for seven-passenger seating in the Touring model, which had two folding rear jump seats.*

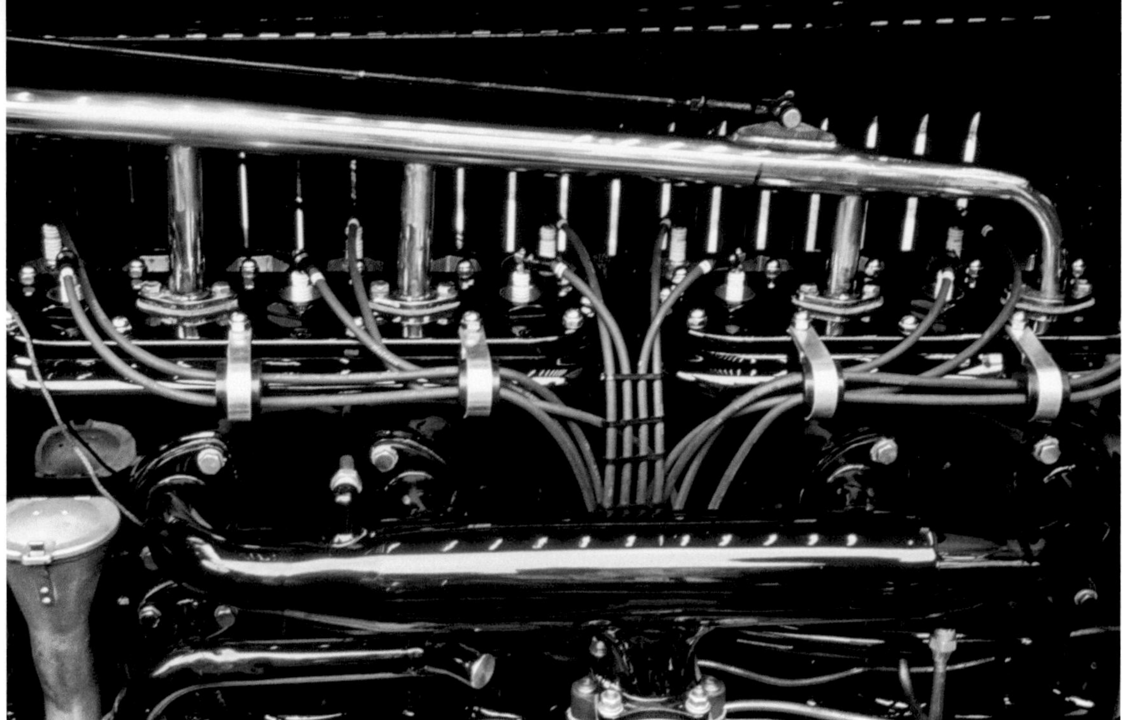

*Packard general manager Alvan Macauley named it the "Dominant Six," Packard's most powerful engine in 1915, developing 82 horsepower and capable of speeds in excess of 70 mph. The handsomely styled engine, designed by chief engineer Jesse Vincent, utilized new heads cast in two blocks of three, with a bore x stroke of 4½ x 5½ inches for a massive swept volume of 525 cubic inches.*

tion, said, "No longer may we ignore the ironical suggestions that have poured in since homicide by motor car has come into prominence in New York. Newspaper pictures of the 'gray murder car' show unmistakably that it is a Packard, an unknowing and innocent accomplice of 'Lefty' Louis, 'Dago Frank' and the rest. Our friends intimate that the lightning like getaway has recommended the Packard to the dark uses of the powers that prey. Jesse James, Dick Turpin and other outlaws of yesterday and the day before used the best horses obtainable . . . The selection of the Packard by the gun men of New York is, we insist, a matter of evolution and no reflection on the integrity of the car." Still, the notoriety didn't hurt Packard sales.

Coachwork was hand crafted in the Packard body shops; the wood framing and wood trim painstakingly machined and hand-polished in the wood shop. Packards leaving East Grand Boulevard were the epitome of hand-crafted luxury. Regardless of the model, body style, or price, every Packard received the same high level of craftsmanship.

This elegant 1915 Model 5-48 seven-passenger Touring is from the Nethercutt Collection in Sylmar, California, and is painted traditional Packard colors: blue and black with yellow trim and wheels, and upholstered in black leather. This stunning open car originally sold for $4,850.

Having reached what many considered to be the epitome of design and engineering for the era, Packard's 4-48 models were virtually unchanged and carried over as the 5-48 in 1915, the year a Packard Six Touring was chosen as pacesetter for the fifth Indianapolis 500 Mile Memorial Day Race. The crowning achievement for the mighty Dominant Six, its role as Packard's flagship, ended that month with the introduction of yet another engineering masterpiece from Jesse Vincent, the all-new Packard Twin Six, America's first 12-cylinder production automobile.

While we can't say you'll feel like a long lost relative of "Lefty" Louis if you get behind the wheel of a Packard Dominant Six, you will experience what it was like to drive the fastest American production car of its day. ◆

# *No.* 35

## Ferrari 250GT Tour de France

### *Ferrari's Legendary Berlinettas*

**THEY WERE CALLED BERLINETTAS** and their story begins in the mid-1950s when Enzo Ferrari began to embrace the duality of road cars and racecars. Ferrari had by then started offering coupes, but a Berlinetta was not a coupe. In Italian, Berlinetta means "little sedan" and the distinction between that and a coupe is simply its purpose. A Berlinetta is meant for racing.

Berlinettas were lighter in weight, a racing advantage often achieved at the expense of comfort and convenience. They had fewer sound deadening materials, thinner body panels, Plexiglas in place of tempered glass, lighter weight carpeting or none at all, and minimum trim. Even bumpers were often discarded. Still, a Berlinetta was roadworthy and could be easily driven on the open road, albeit with a greater degree of attention to engine revs, coolant temperature, speed, and the elements, which took on much greater volume within the confines of a cockpit almost devoid of soundproofing.

Construction of the TdF was handled by Carrozzeria Scaglietti and based on a design by Pinin Farina. The heady V12 engine began with an output of 240 horsepower, which was increased to 260 horsepower by the end of production. In 1959, a one-off short wheelbase Tdf was built for the 24 Hours of Le Mans. This car,

*The design for the 250 GT Berlinetta Tour de France followed the Mercedes-Benz 300 SLR accident at Le Mans in 1955. This tragedy marked a turning point for sports car racing, which had progressed to where competition sports cars were closer to Grand Prix cars. As a result, the Fédération Internationale de l'Automobile created new racing classes and with help from Pinin Farina, Ferrari was ready to compete in the new GT category by 1956 with the 250 GT (Grand Touring) Berlinetta Tour de France.*

*The second series Tour de France was an even more astounding car with bold new styling and distinctive high-crowned front fenders and rear tail fins. The TdF remained in production until 1959. The example shown from the Ron Busuttil collection was built in 1958.*

named the 250 GT Interim, would foreshadow the 250 GT SWB Berlinetta's debut at October's Paris Motor Show.

### THE 250 GT LINEAGE

The 250 GT designations represent the longest running road and race series in Ferrari history. From 1954 through to 1959, Ferrari manufactured roughly 100 purpose-built Berlinettas for endurance sports car racing. After the Ferraris took the top three places at the 1957 Tour de France, for which the cars were named, they continued to prove their versatility in numerous road races becoming the car of choice among top drivers.

### THE RACE

Starting in Nice and ending five days and 3,345 miles later in Paris, the Tour de France was one of the most important races of its day. In true road rally fashion established by such historic competitions as the Targa Florio and Mille Miglia, the Tour de France tested both durability and versatility through open road rally-style stages, six circuit races (Comminges, Le Mans, Rouen, Rheims, St. Etienne, and Montlhéry),

DRIVING THIS LEGEND DEMANDS SKILL, BUT THE REWARD IS A QUICK THROTTLE, A RESOLUTE EXHAUST NOTE AS THE ENGINE'S TEMPO INCREASES AND THE FERRARI'S AGILE HANDLING COMES INTO PLAY. HERE ARE THE VISCERAL SENSATIONS KNOWN TO FAMED DRIVERS WHO HURTLED AROUND RACE COURSES OR CHALLENGED THE MEXICAN DESERT IN THE CARRERA PANAMERICANA.

two hill climbs (Mt. Ventoux and Peyresounde) and a drag race (a 500-meter course at Aix-les-Bains). The Tour de France demanded speed, reliability, regularity, and stamina from both the teams and their cars. In 1956 only 37 of 103 starters finished the Tour! One of them was the stylish and quick Alfonso de Portago and co-pilot Gunnar Nelson, driving an early version of the 1956 250 GT into 1st place overall after winning outright five of the six circuit races on the Tour. Second to Portago was none other than Stirling Moss, driving a factory-backed Mercedes-Benz 300 SL.

## UNDER THE HOOD

The common link between all 250 GTs was Gioacchino Colombo's unfailing 3-liter, V12 engine. This was the smaller of two V12 engines developed by Ferrari for use in road and racecars and was required to meet new restrictions on engine size mandated after the 1955 Le Mans incident. The F.I.A. imposed

*The rear end design of the second series TdF gave the cars a distinctive appearance.*

*Under the hood, the Tour de France was all business with the 250 GT engine delivering 240 horsepower at 7,000 rpm. The V12 breathed through three Weber 36 DCF carburetors.*

the 3-liter limit in an attempt to curb high speed accidents. Although Ferrari's 3-liter engine was still good for 230 to 250 horsepower using three down-draft Weber carburetors, the top speeds of the previous years, often as great as 180 mph, could no longer be reached.

The TdF used this engine in combination with a long wheelbase chassis until the shorter 94.5-inch chassis of the SWB Berlinetta replaced it in 1959. Each chassis received a hand-crafted body, most of which came from Sergio Scaglietti's shop in Modena. Scaglietti, as much sculptor as coachbuilder, may be credited with much of this model's aesthetic appeal, softening some of Pinin Farina's more harsh lines to create a unitary design that may be fairly described as "voluptuous."

Progressive development and handcrafted bodies meant that no two 250 GT Berlinettas were exactly the same. Differences were incorporated into the body from year to year, with subtle details such as sliding or wind-up windows, cowled or covered or plain headlights, and varied hood louvers distinguishing each car. The first TdFs were modeled after the 250 MM, both having the same general proportions and wraparound rear windscreen. Later changes to body included a smaller rear windscreen, the addition of louvers on the C-pillar for cockpit cooling, and more pronounced rear fenders. In 1958 Scaglietti's design evolved slightly. Headlights were recessed into the front fenders and covered with plexiglass fairings. Three slot front fender vents were featured. The rear fender peaks and taillights became more prominent and the greenhouse sail panel had a single vent to exhaust air from the closed interior. This style has become accepted as the definitive iteration of the 250 GT Tour de France, an instantly recognized form.

In 1958, the Tour de France also benefited from numerous mechanical improvements, the most important of which was a new gearbox with centrally located shift lever. Many internal features of the engine were strengthened and there were new valves, new crankshaft, stronger connecting rods, and revised cylinder heads and intake manifold.

The appropriateness of the appellation "Tour de France" for these cars became even more obvious when in 1958 Gendebien/Bianchi repeated their overall victory, this time followed by Trintignant/Picard (again) and Da Silva Ramos/Estager in 3rd, all in 250 GT Ferraris. The magnitude of these accomplishments is apparent from the fact that in 1957 only 23 of 72 starters reached the finish line in the Tour; in 1958 it was only 21 of 60!

Although many great Ferraris have driven down the road from Maranello, few can boast the rich history of the Tour de France—a car that even after half a century ranks among the most coveted of all 250 GTs. ◆

*The Tour de France was a sleek, closed car designed specifically for racing. By design, a Berlinetta is a lightweight, streamlined body trimmed for racing—this being the distinguishing characteristic between a Berlinetta and a traditional coupe. The first series Tour de France, such as this 1956 model owned today by Richard Gent, were unlike any Ferrari competition sports cars.*

# *No.* 36

## 1939 DELAHAYE 165 V12

### *French Curves*

**AS SURELY AS THE BRUSH OF A GREAT MASTER** on canvas or a symphony penned by Mozart, the automotive creations of French designers in the 1930s and postwar early 1940s were works of art, portraits in steel sculptured by the hands of artisans and set into motion by gallant engineers with unlimited imagination. This was Paris in the classic era, the very core of international automotive design and home to one of France's oldest automakers, Delahaye.

### THE CHANGING FACE OF SUCCESS

Since 1906 Delahaye had been guided by one man, Charles Weiffenbach. As chairman and having sole discretionary power (such power coming after two decades of success and profits), he was faced in the 1930s with a declining economy, the first France had seen since the early post-World War I years. Delahaye had succeeded on its reputation and the quality of products after the war, but now as America's Great Depression swept over Europe, Weiffenbach was faced with a nation divided between the very rich and the very poor. Average Frenchmen were not buying new cars, at least not Delahayes. Weiffenbach decided it was best to cater to France's privileged class and leave mass production to automakers like Renault and Peugeot who were better suited to the task. Despite its age and years of success, Delahaye was a small company compared to many of its European contemporaries. In 1933 Weiffenbach set out to make Delahaye a leader in the luxury and sports racing class, and to do so in the face of competition from Ettore Bugatti, Louis Delage, Alfa Romeo, and Mercedes-Benz. Weiffenbach nevertheless cast Delahaye's fate to the wind and at the 1933 Paris Auto Salon unveiled the

*The coachwork designed by Joseph Figoni for the Delahaye 165 V12 was the most stylish design of 1939. Had it not been for the beginning of World War II, it is likely that the Figoni V12s would have been among the most sought-after cars of the year.*

*From the rear it is evident how the sweep of the fenders totally enclosed the body. The front skirted fenders had to be wide enough to allow the wheels to turn, thus accentuating the width of the body. Taillights were limited to the two small lamps on either side of the number plate.*

*Superluxe,* which was powered by a 3.2-liter six-cylinder engine delivering 120 horsepower. The car featured an independent front suspension and large self-adjusting brakes. By design, it was a chassis that could be bodied for touring or fitted with lightweight coachwork suited to sports car competition. A year later this became the Type 135, equipped with a slightly larger 3.5-liter engine and an array of coachwork that made the new Delahaye suitable for everything from cruising along the Champs Élysées to screeching down the Mulsanne Straight at Le Mans. With coachwork from the leading design houses in Paris—Figoni, Saoutchik, and Chapron—the Type 135 would become one of the most desirable and luxurious automobiles in Europe. Weiffenbach and Delahaye had prevailed.

In competition, the company was equally successful in five seasons, including a 1st in the 1934 Monte Carlo Rally and the Coupe des Alps; a 3rd overall at Le Mans in 1935 (making it the first French car to finish); a sweeping 2nd, 4th, 5th, and 7th in the

**THE WIND-CHISELED LINES OF THE DELAHAYE V12 SURROUND YOU WITH ONE OF THE GREATEST AUTOMOBILES EVER DESIGNED. IT IS POWERED BY A MASSIVE V12 THAT TAKES ITS ORDERS FROM A GEARBOX NO LARGER THAN A GOLF BALL AND SHIFTER THAT IS MOVED BY THUMB AND FOREFINGER ALONE. ON THE OPEN ROAD THE ENGINE ROARS, NOT SO MUCH A CLAMOR FROM BENEATH THE HOOD, BUT A LACK OF WIND NOISE TO DISTRACT AS THE AIR FLOWS SMOOTHLY OVER THE FENDERS AND SWIRLS AROUND THE COCKPIT.**

1936 Automobile Club of France Grand Prix; and an overall victory at Le Mans in 1938. The following year Weiffenbach took the boldest step yet.

## THE CYLINDER WARS

In America, Great Britain, and Europe, automakers had thrown caution to the wind in the early 1930s, building cars not with six- or eight-cylinder engines but with twelve and even sixteen cylinders. Though late to the game, Delahaye joined the cylinder wars in 1939 with a winning design introduced at the Paris Salon. The new Type 165 chassis, equipped with a V12 engine, was clothed in a cabriolet body designed and built by the master of aerodynamics, Joseph Figoni. The styling was similar to Figoni's Type 135 bodies, but given the proportions of the massive cabriolet, the 165 appeared larger than life, literally and figuratively. Only one example was completed, and a second non-running display car shown at the Paris Salon.

Bodied as a two-seater, a competition formula less common as Delahayes were generally designed to accommodate four passengers, the Figoni Cabriolet had a seductive aerodynamic motif. With just a trace of windshield, chromed speed lines along the hood and doors, and Figoni's bold, elliptical teardrop fenders, the 165 was an image of captured motion, as though being stretched rearward by the force of its speed.

The interior was upholstered in white ostrich contrasted by red piping, the instruments gathered in a chromed-trimmed red fascia at the center of the dashboard. The car was equipped with the popular Cotal pre-selector transmission mounted to the left side of the steering column. It simply astounded everyone at the 1939 Paris salon. Had Europe not been overcome by war in September, the Delahaye Type 165 might well have become the most coveted new model of 1939.

Monsieur Charles, as Weiffenbach was known around the Delahaye works, had accomplished nearly all of his goals by 1939. When the war in Europe ended in 1945, Delahaye roared back with a stunning line of cars fitted with the finest coachwork that Figoni and his contemporary, Henri Chapron, could build.

Delahaye and Delage, which had been acquired by Weiffenbach in 1935, soon discovered the world had changed too much during the war. Neither company could survive in the postwar turmoil; there simply were not enough customers. Their market had always been small, and now too small. By 1951 production had declined to just 77 cars and three years later the company was taken over by Hotchkiss—and Hotchkiss didn't build cars.

The two 1939 Delahaye V12s survived the war and the second car now has an engine under its long length of hood. Both are in private collections and a trip around the block in either one of them would be as unforgettable as their debut in Paris in 1939. ◆

Hollywood
HORNET

# No. 37

## 1953 Hudson Hornet Hollywood Hardtop

### *Hudson's Hot Rod*

**THE 1950S WAS A GREAT TIME** to be buying a new car. There weren't as many choices as today, but every car was distinctive, and just about every one of them was made in the USA. In the fifties, one name stood out among those who followed AAA and NASCAR racing—Hudson. As far back as the early 1910s, they had been known for speed and endurance. In April 1916, a Hudson set the one-mile straightaway stock car speed record at 102.5 mph at Daytona Beach. In May, at Sheepshead Bay, the 24-hour stock car record fell to a Hudson turning an average speed of 74.8 mph, a record that would not be surpassed until 1931! A Hudson also set the world's first double transcontinental record, driving from San Francisco to New York and back in September 1916.

After World War II, as American servicemen began returning home, one of their first priorities was the purchase of a new car. There hadn't been a new car available in the U.S. since early in 1942. Hudson wasted little time returning to motorsports competition, blazing a trail through early NASCAR outings and in AAA sanctioned racing. In the hands of skilled tuners, the Hudson Hornet's 308-cubic-inch L-head six could be urged to deliver up to 210 horsepower, and the factory even offered special "severe-usage" options designed for racing. For stock car competition, Hornets were among the best built cars of the day with responsive handling, quick steering, and an almost unbreakable suspension.

*The Hudson Hornet Hollywood Hardtop was one of the most exciting new models of 1953. This is among the rarest of Hudson models. Only 910 were built in 1953.*

*The most elegant of the Hudson Hornets was the Brougham. The handsome convertible models sold for $2,500. The cars were so sleek and low to the ground they looked as if they had been customized by George Barris.*

Hudson Hornets were available in four body styles: a sleek four-door sedan, a two-door convertible Brougham, a two-door Club Coupe (a favorite for racing), and the glamorous Hollywood Hardtop.

All new Hudson models featured the manufacturer's exclusive "step-down" chassis design placing the entire passenger compartment within the frame members. This provided exceptional passenger safety, a lower overall height for the car of 60⅜ inches, and all without sacrificing headroom. The "step-down" design also lowered the Hudson's center of gravity, making the cars less likely to roll over, one of the reasons they were so popular with stock car drivers.

Proven in competition for three years, the Hornets used an A-arm and coil spring independent front suspension and rugged solid axle rear with semi-elliptical leaf springs, direct-acting shock absorbers at all four corners, a dual-acting front stabilizer, and a lateral stabilizer in the rear. For the 1950s, the Hudson Hornet was very likely the best handling and best built American car in its price class.

Whether a Hollywood Hardtop or a sporty convertible, at just a little over 17 feet in length and riding on a 124-inch wheelbase, the average Hornet weighed in at around 3,600 pounds. Both of the two-door models left little to be desired, either from within or under the hood. Powering the cars was a Hudson 308-cubic-inch, inline six-cylinder side-valve engine mixing fuel through a Carter two-barrel carburetor. Hudson's Twin-H option, (twin carburetors) was added in 1952 and offered through 1954, as was a dual-range HydraMatic transmission in place of the

TUNE THE RADIO, LOWER THE WINDOWS, AND REST YOUR LEFT ARM ON TOP OF THE DOOR (SHIRT SLEEVE ROLLED UP, OF COURSE), AND IT'S SATURDAY NIGHT, ANY NIGHT OF THE WEEK. THE HUDSON HORNET IS A RIDE BACK IN TIME WITH ITS FIFTIES' STYLING AND HEADY 308 STRAIGHT SIX. WANT TO KNOW WHAT IT WAS LIKE TO BE JUNIOR JOHNSON IN THE 1950S? THIS IS WHERE YOU START.

manual column shift. The Twin-H helped give racers the competitive edge and for those who wanted a real thrill ride around town it was a must-have option.

From 1951 through 1953, output from the L-head six with the single Carter was a substantial 145 horsepower at 3,800 rpm, 160 horsepower with the Twin-H. Horsepower was raised to a vigorous 160 at 3,800 rpm and 170 horsepower with Twin-H in 1954, the last year for the Hudson line. It was a grand way to go out. On May 1, 1954, Hudson merged with Nash to form the American Motors Corporation. While the merger was the road to survival for the two automakers, it was a dead end street for Hudson. On May 27, Hudson employees were notified that production was being moved to the Nash automobile factory in Kenosha, Wisconsin. When the 1954 model run ended on October 30, 1954, at Hudson's Jefferson Avenue plant in Detroit, so, too, did an era in automotive history. ◆

*All Hornets were powered by the H-145, 308-cubic-inch inline six-cylinder side-valve engine. They featured an exclusive chrome-alloy cylinder block and "power Dome" aluminum head. Output was a substantial 145 horsepower. In 1954, the bore was increased, as was compression, and the engine poured out a rousing 160 horsepower and another 10 with the Twin-H (twin carburetors). When tuned for competition, the engines could put out up to 210 horsepower.*

PT-97 15

# *No.* 38

## 1936 HISPANO-SUIZA J-12

### *France and the Cylinder Wars*

**ON ANY LIST OF GREAT AUTOMOBILES YOU** will find the name Hispano-Suiza. Not only coveted by car collectors, Hispano-Suiza is equally regarded among vintage aircraft enthusiasts. Established in 1898, the company continued to produce automobiles until 1937, with the majority of its luxury cars manufactured in France beginning in 1919.

### THE ROYAL RIDE

Hispano-Suiza was one of the few automakers in history to have royal recognition, having been blessed with the patronage of Spain's King Alfonso XIII. The company even named a 1907 model in his honor. The Suiza (Swiss) portion of the name has nothing to do with Switzerland other than the country being the home of the company's chief engineer, Marc Birkigt, one of the greatest mechanical minds of the early twentieth century. Under his leadership, the firm prospered despite changing principal owners several times, two reorganizations, the establishment of a Paris branch in 1911, and the relocation of automotive operations to France in 1919. Although the original factories in Barcelona and Madrid continued to build more traditional cars until the end of World War II, nearly all of the legendary cars to bear the Hispano-Suiza name and flying stork mascot, including the magnificent J-12, would come from the French branch at Bois-Colombes.

Hispano-Suiza automobiles had established a reputation for mechanical durability based upon Birkigt's design for an overhead cam, light-alloy six-cylinder aero engine so well engineered that it would remain in production for both aircraft and

*One of the most beautiful and powerful automobiles of the 1930s was the Hispano-Suiza J-12. Many of the custom bodies were constructed in Belgium by Carrossier d'Ieteren Frérès.*

*This regal 1936 J-12 Convertible Victoria was capable of reaching more than 100 mph when the driver desired to travel ". . . at aircraft speed in the open."*

automobiles, almost without change, from 1918 until the early 1930s. More than 50,000 Hispano-Suiza engines were produced, mostly for aircraft.

By the 1930s, competition from American automaker Cadillac, which had introduced both V16 and V12 engines, convinced Birkigt to double the capacity of his reliable six and introduce a new and very competitive V12 with a massive swept volume of 9,424 cubic centimeters (572 cubic inches) and an output of 200 horsepower at 3,000 rpm. A later version, equipped with a high-performance crankshaft, delivered a breathtaking 250 horsepower (65 more than a Cadillac V16!) and was easily capable of exceeding 100 mph. A J-12 with almost anything short of a limousine body could clock zero to 60 mph in an average of 12 seconds.

To make the cars as appealing as possible, Hispano-Suiza offered four wheelbase lengths, a 146-inch "light" chassis, a 134½-inch "short" chassis for more sporting coachwork, a 150-inch stretch for sedans, and the immense 157¾-inch "long" chassis for limousines, town cars, and broughams. The Convertible Victoria pictured was mounted on the "light" chassis and coachbuilt in Belgium by d'Ieteren Frérès for William A. M. Burden, the great-great-grandson of Cornelius Vanderbilt. During WWII Burden was appointed U.S. Secretary of Commerce, and in 1959 the U.S. Ambassador to Belgium. The design of this car is similar to several J-12 models produced by d'Ieteren Frérès, which was the principal coachbuilder for Hispano-Suiza in the 1930s.

Although automobiles made Hispano-Suiza

WHETHER FROM THE DRIVER'S SEAT OR THE BACK SEAT, EVERY VIEW IS THE BEST SEAT IN THE HOUSE. AS YOU ACCELERATE, THE BOOMING V12 SOUNDS LIKE AN AIRCRAFT ENGINE. THE WIND SWIRLS AROUND YOUR HEAD, THE SCENTS IN THE AIR INVIGORATE, AND THERE IS THE SENSATION OF TOURING DOWN SOME ANCIENT EUROPEAN ROADWAY.

famous, the design and production of aircraft engines had always been the company's primary trade. It was also the cause of the French division's demise during the Second World War. The Bois-Colombes factory had been converted to build V12 aero engines shortly after the beginning of the war in 1939, and following the invasion of France in June 1940, the works were confiscated by the Nazis. During the war, the factories in Spain continued to produce cars, but by 1945 Hispano-Suiza was out of the automobile business.

Though few in number, the J-12s were the equal of the mightiest motorcars built in Europe and America—the Cadillac V12 and V16, Lincoln, Packard, Franklin, Auburn, and Pierce-Arrow V12s, and the mighty supercharged Duesenbergs and 540K Mercedes-Benz. Hispano-Suiza only managed to build around 100 J-12 models between 1931 and 1937, but it's easily one of the greatest automobiles of the twentieth century. ◆

*One of the most powerful engines of its time, the aero engine-based V12 in the Hispano-Suiza J-12 could deliver up to 250 horsepower. The only production engine of the 1930s that could better the J-12 was the supercharged Duesenberg straight eight.*

18-258
X 32 WASHINGTON

*No.* 39

# 1932 Lincoln KB V12

## *The Ultimate Ford*

**THE LINCOLN MODEL K WAS EDSEL B. FORD'S** treatise on design and luxury. Even the model designation was Edsel's choosing. In 1931, the "K" marked the beginning of a new era for Lincoln, which had been in the Ford Motor Company family since its acquisition from Henry and Wilfred Leland in January 1922. It was not until 1931, however, that Lincoln truly ascended to the role Edsel Ford had envisioned for nearly a decade.

As an independent automaker, Lincoln had been founded by the elder Leland after his departure from Cadillac and General Motors in 1917. Following a long and heated series of debates with William C. Durant over America's involvement in World War I (Leland wanted to build aircraft engines, Durant, a devout pacifist, did not), the founder and number one man at Cadillac stepped down to form the Liberty Engine Company. Between August 1917 and January 1919, Leland manufactured more than 6,000 400-horsepower V12 aircraft engines. Few, however, were actually put into use during the war. The role for Leland's engines was actually greater than he had imagined during his arguments with Durant. They were used to establish the Army Air Corps and later, the U.S. Air Mail Service. Unfortunately for Henry Martyn Leland, peacetime demands for 12-cylinder aircraft engines fell well short of expectations. With his Detroit factories idled and more than 6,000 employees at the ready, Leland decided to return to his first love, building automobiles. In

*A stately car from the front, the powerful Lincoln grille provided a commanding visage whether ahead of a coupe or a limousine body style. The new V12-powered KB Lincolns were intended to level the playing field with Cadillac, which had both V12 and V16 models. (Wellington Morton collection)*

*Built on a massive 145-inch wheelbase chassis, the Judkins Coupe was a very large two-seater! To bring this nearly 18-foot-long car to a stop, Lincoln used vacuum servo-assisted mechanical drum brakes. The brake system was adjustable from the steering column for summer and winter driving.*

1919, design work began on an all-new American motorcar to be named after the nation's sixteenth president and Henry Leland's boyhood hero, Abraham Lincoln.

## ENGINEERING VS. STYLE

At Cadillac, Leland had established a world renowned reputation for precision manufacturing, and his intention with Lincoln was to build what he termed the "Permanent Motorcar," an automobile so well built that it would last for decades with only routine maintenance. Early advertisements for Lincoln Motor Cars made mention of the highly respected Leland name, stating in bold type, LELAND-BUILT. To those who remembered the quality and durability of prewar Cadillacs and the power of the Liberty engines that forged America's first Arsenal of Democracy, this was an invitation to purchase a great new motorcar.

In every respect the Lincoln was overbuilt and over-engineered to last. Alas, when the Lincoln finally arrived in September 1920, its antiquated coachwork, designed by Leland's son-in-law Angus Woodbridge, fell short of expectations and the cars were widely ridiculed by dealers and customers alike. As an engineer Leland was almost without equal, but when it came to deciding upon the cataloged coachwork that would fit atop his magnificent chassis, he had a far too pragmatic engineer's eye.

By November 1921 Lincoln was in receivership. It was more than staid body styling and slow sales that brought the Lelands to their bitter crossroads. With only 675 cars sold in 1921, a dissident group of board members was demanding the dissolution of the company. Leland sought additional financing from the New York banks and would have had it were it not for the untimely arrival of a demand for payment from Uncle Sam for war-profits taxes in the amount of $4.5 million. This is what brought Lincoln to its knees. In 1921 the entire Lincoln Motor Company was offered for less than had been spent to engineer the Model L. It was an opportunity for someone to step in and buy a company for a fraction of what it had been worth, and Henry Ford was nothing if not an opportunist. And then there was the element of retribution. It was Leland who forced Henry Ford out of the Henry Ford Company in 1902 and turned it into the Cadillac Automobile Company. Thus, there was a certain degree of frostiness in the dealings which turned Lincoln into the new luxury car division of Ford Motor Company in 1922. By June, the Lelands were gone and 28-year-old Edsel Bryant Ford assumed the presidency of the Lincoln Motor Company. Things were about to shift into top gear.

## EDSEL AT THE HELM

From the late 1920s and up until the end of the 1930s, Cadillac owned the "prestige" name in limousines and town cars, but Lincolns were generally the most attractively styled of the two rival marques. This was due, for the most part, to Edsel Ford, whose exceptional sense of style guided the company's selection of coachwork and coachbuilders. Edsel was a stylist at heart, and when a particular custom body appealed to his

*The 1932 Lincoln could be ordered with a Motorola radio. The tuner is mounted to the left of the steering wheel, while the receiver and speaker are mounted against the firewall. A simple yet elegant instrument panel with blackface instruments contrasted against a beautiful engine-turned fascia.*

**THE LINCOLN KB COUPE WAS A "BANKER'S HOT ROD" WITH A MIGHTY 150-HORSEPOWER V12 UNDER THE HOOD. ACCELERATION ISN'T HEAD SNAPPING, BUT AT HIGHWAY SPEEDS AND UP TO THE MAGIC 100 MPH MARK, THE KB IS SOLID AND ALMOST SILENT. MAKE NO MISTAKE; THIS IS A BIG CAR, EVEN IF IT IS DESIGNED TO SEAT ONLY TWO.**

aesthetic tastes, he would contract for its production on a semi-custom basis. As a result, Lincoln customers had access to body styles that would otherwise have been limited to and priced as full custom jobs. By the end of the 1920s he was poised to make Lincoln not only one of the most successful, but most beautiful luxury cars on the American road.

From 1921 to 1939, the J. B. Judkins coachworks produced a total of 5,904 custom and series-built-custom bodies for Lincoln, more than any other custom body builder in America. Judkins bodies were pictured in lavish color catalogs displaying each of the custom and semi-custom bodies available from Lincoln. These were sometimes referred to as "catalog customs." The example pictured was completed by Judkins in Amesbury, Massachusetts, on January 2, 1932. It was built as a Salon exhibition car and shown at the Drake Hotel in Chicago, the Biltmore Hotel in Los Angeles, and the Palace Hotel in San Francisco. The car was priced at $5,415. Approximately 23 KB coupes were built by Judkins in 1932, a dozen of which were of this specific body style.

Edsel's influence and unquestioned knowledge of styling was felt at every coachbuilder supplying bodies to Lincoln. Judkins ended up with a large portion of Lincoln's small and mid-sized series-built custom bodies, which included Berlines, sedans, and coupes, such as the handsome 1932 KB model. Judkins continued to produce "Catalog Custom" Coupes well into the 1930s for Lincoln's new Model K, and KA and KB chassis. ◆

*Opposite. Under the KB Lincoln hood was a massive 150-horsepower, 447.9-cubic-inch, fork and blade, sixty-degree V12 weighing a little over half a ton! The engine was coupled to a 3-speed synchromesh transmission.*

# No. 40

## 1965 Lamborghini 350 GT

### *The First Great Raging Bull*

**BY THE 1960S, FERRARI HAD BEEN** an established manufacturer of race and road cars for almost 20 years. The other legendary Italian sports car builders, Maserati and Alfa Romeo, had been producing racecars and sports cars for more than half a century. Lamborghini was a virtually unknown marque in 1965 unless one happened to be an Italian farmer. Up until the debut of the company's

FERRUCCIO LAMBORGHINI'S ORIGINAL PLAN, TO ONE-UP FERRARI, COMES THROUGH IN THE 350 GT'S LUXURIOUS LEATHER INTERIOR, FULL COMPLEMENT OF INSTRUMENTS, AND 270-HORSEPOWER V12. IT IS AN AGILE AND PREDICTABLE CAR, " . . . MUCH LESS DEMANDING TO DRIVE THAN A FERRARI," WROTE *CAR AND DRIVER* IN 1966. DRIVING A 350 GT IS ONE OF LIFE'S LITTLE PLEASURES.

first sports car in 1963, Lamborghini had only built farm tractors; hardly the credentials for entering the highly competitive Italian sports car market. The 1963 prototype was mechanically sound but aesthetically less than pleasing. Almost there, but not quite. Lamborghini had tried to combine too many different styling aspects into his first model and ended up with the proverbial camel instead of a horse, or in this case a bull.

*After a restyling by Carrozzeria Touring in 1963, the first Lamborghini emerged the following year as a stunning GT sports car. (Jerry J. Moore collection)*

*Lamborghini made the best possible use of leather throughout the passenger compartment and particularly in the dashboard design. The GT 350 was far more luxurious than a Ferrari.*

As many automakers in both Italy and throughout Europe had done since the 1920s, they turned to Carrozzeria Touring in Milan for help when a body design needed to be improved upon or entirely rethought. Ferrari had done it in 1949, so too had BMW in the late 1930s, and this was the prescribed course for Ferruccio Lamborghini to follow after the failure of the 350 GTV in 1963. A year later, Touring had taken "almost there" and turned it into a design that four decades later still turns heads and quickens the pulse of anyone who sees it.

Touring used its patented *Superleggera* construction—an aluminum body mounted over a structural skeleton of steel tubes. This resulted in a strong yet lighter weight body, a technique that had been proven by Touring-bodied racecars since the 1930s. The trendy pop-up headlights of the 350 GTV were eliminated and replaced by two sleek oval nacelles containing single large headlamps. The large glass fastback evolved from the GTV worked in concert with the crowned Touring fender line. Overall, it was the same car but beautifully refined.

The Bizzarrini-designed V12, with four overhead camshafts, six horizontal Weber carburetors (the GTV had used vertical carburetors), wet sump lubrication, and a pair of Marelli distributors, delivered a sensational 270 horsepower at 7,000 rpm transferred to the ground via a ZF 5-speed transmission.

With a low, wide stance, the 350 GT measured just 48½ inches to the roof, 67 inches across, and rode on a short 100.4-inch wheelbase. The Lamborghini's fully independent suspension, utilizing coil springs, telescopic shock absorbers, and heavy-duty Girling disc brakes at all four corners, endowed the GT 350 with handling to match its appearance. In 1965 the engine was further improved by enlarging the bore from 77 millimeters to 86 millimeters, increasing the V12's swept volume to 4.0 liters and output to 320 horsepower at 6,500 rpm. Regrettably, Lamborghini only built 143 of them. Today they are among the rarest and most coveted of the cars from Bologna. ◆

*Above. The immense backlight gave the 350 GT a striking rear visage, as did the short deck and trunk.*

*Below. Former Ferrari engineer Giotto Bizzarrini designed the first Lamborghini V12 engine. The versions used in the 350 GT featured four overhead camshafts, six horizontal Weber carburetors, wet sump lubrication, and a pair of Marelli distributors. Output was a sensational 270 horsepower.*

# *No.* 41

## 1960 MGA Twin Cam

### *The Sportsman's Sports Car*

**DESIGNER CECIL KIMBER AND THE** Morris Garage (MG) had provided a wellspring of ideas since the 1930s, when MG became synonymous with the term "sports car." MG's four-square two-seaters established the standard that other British makes such as AC and Jaguar followed in the late 1930s. And it was the prewar MG two-seaters that caught the eye of American soldiers returning home after World War II. In America, the sporty MG TC and TD models became popular with would-be sports car racers and were paramount among the models owned by the founding members of the Sports Car Club of America. Jaguar's superb XK-120 followed on the heels of the postwar MG models, and from both came the inspiration for the 1953 Corvette.

The MG TC and improved TD models had done well throughout the late 1940s and early 1950s, and when modified for competition and fitted with special oversized valves, milled heads, domed pistons, and higher compression ratios to extract every fragment of horsepower from the production line four-cylinder motors, the cars were very competitive. But by the mid-1950s they were fast becoming the victims of their own obsolescence. Even the more modern TF model was a short-lived success. MG was the last import sports car carrying vestiges of prewar design, with the exception of Morgan, which had made building old-style cars their hallmark. Porsche, Alfa Romeo, Jaguar, Mercedes-Benz, and even Chevrolet had passed MG in styling and performance by 1955, when the company finally came around and introduced an all-new sports car bearing the MG octagon.

*As a J production racer, the Twin Cam was a successful car, bringing countless victories to MG in the hands of amateur and professional race drivers the world over. As a street car, the Twin Cam was a handful for most owners, far more difficult to manage than the 1500 and later Mark II 1600s, and subject to burned or holed pistons if not kept scrupulously in tune.*

## BREAKING NEW GROUND

The styling for the MGA was based on a 1951 racecar driven by George Phillips in the 24 Hours of Le Mans. It had been built by MG using TD running gear and a lightweight two-seat racecar-style body. So different was the appearance of Phillip's racer that it must have been difficult to believe that it was actually a TD underneath.

A year later a road-going version of the Phillips car had been proposed to MG's parent company BMC as a replacement for the aging T Series, but BMC had already given the go-ahead to sister company Austin-Healey to build the new Type 100, a car not too dissimilar from the 1955 MGA. When it became clear to management that the modestly redesigned MG TF was a bit of a lame duck, they approved the MGA. Before the official launch in 1955, three aluminum-bodied prototypes of the new sports car were entered at Le Mans. Fortunately for MG, they acquitted themselves well, finishing 5th and 6th in their class. A few months after the race, on September 22, 1955, the company unveiled the MGA at the Frankfurt Auto Show. It was a testament to MG's wisdom that the cars already had a competition background the day they were introduced!

From the very beginning, the MGA was lauded as an instant success by the world's motoring press. In America, *Road & Track* wrote, "Early enthusiasm for its appearance can now be augmented by the knowledge of its very surprising performance. Anybody who likes anything about sports cars will be more

*Opposite. The basic BMC "B" type block used for the MGA was increased to a swept volume of 96.906 cubic inches. Combined with the double overhead cam head and a compression ratio of 9.9:1, the Twin Cam's output shot up to a maximum 107 horsepower at 6,500 rpm. Off the right side of the head (left from this view) is a log-type manifold supporting two H6 S.U. carburetors.*

*Below. Bodies for the MGA, the last to be produced as a separate unit from the chassis, utilized both steel and aluminum panels in their construction. The doors, trunk lid, and hood were of the latter lightweight, rust-free alloy.*

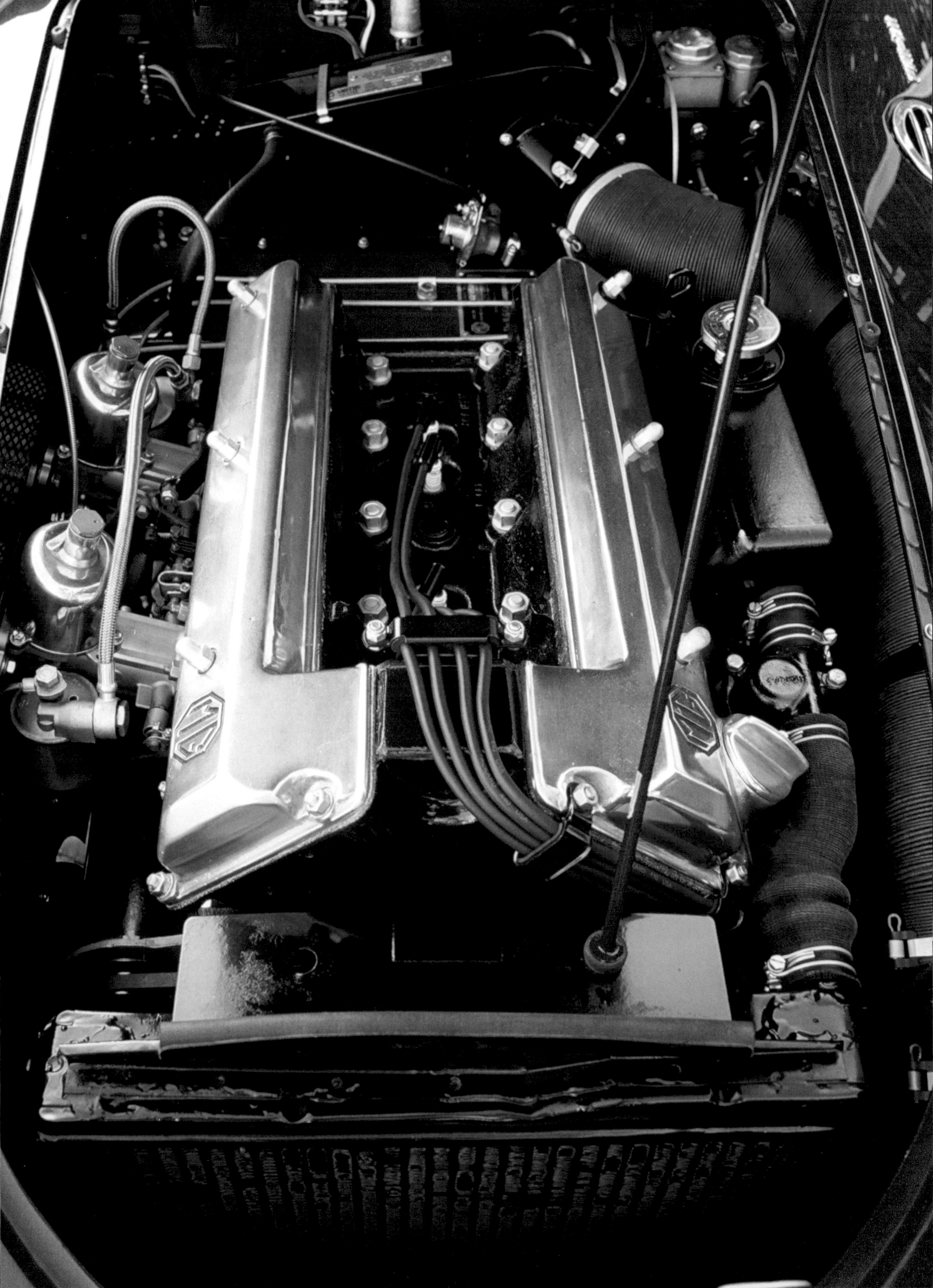

than pleased with the new MG." In *Sports Car Illustrated*, the never overly gracious Griff Borgeson wrote, ". . . basically safe, friendly, likeable car—a genuine well-built sports machine at a price that can't be considered anything but reasonable and fair." High praise from Borgeson!

Sports car enthusiasts wholeheartedly agreed, making the MGA the most popular sports car ever built by the time it went out of production in June 1962. Over seven years, MG sold more than 100,000 MGAs, including a limited production of 2,111 Twin Cam roadsters and coupes, built from September 1958 through June 1960.

DRIVING AN MGA TWIN CAM MAKES EVEN A RUN AROUND THE BLOCK FEEL LIKE A ROAD RALLY. THE CLOSE PROXIMITY OF THE DASH PUTS YOU WITHIN HAND'S REACH OF EVERY CONTROL. STEERING IS QUICK; THE DOHC ENGINE TURNS ON THE POWER EARLY AND KEEPS IT COMING, WHILE THE RACE-PROVEN SUSPENSION MAINTAINS A SOLID FOOTING ON THE ROAD. THE TWIN CAM IS AN EXHILARATING CAR TO DRIVE. MECHANIC NOT INCLUDED.

## TWO CAMS ARE BETTER THAN ONE

The Twin Cam cars had a larger displacement engine with a swept volume of 1,588 cubic centimeters or 96.906 cubic inches. The double overhead cam head (twin cam) gave the engine and additional 1,500 rpm at the top end. Combined with a new compression ratio of 9.9:1 and a pair of H6 S.U. carburetors, the MGA Twin Cam was a race-ready car right out of the box. Where the standard pushrod MGA motors began to taper off, the Twin Cam version was just starting to belt out its newfound power with the horsepower rating shooting up from 76 to 98 horsepower in the space between 4,000 and 5,000 rpm. At the limit, output was 107 horsepower at 6,500 revs.

More than just a hopped-up model with a larger engine, the Twin Cam MGAs were a differed breed of car, one more temperamental and demanding of a driver and mechanic with enough skill to drive and maintain them. The Twin Cam was a difficult car to live with but a great car to race. ◆

RPM
FUEL
TEMPERATURE
MAX
DEMIST

49
L'OR.SCHELL
SPL.
RENÉ LE BÈGUE
49

# *No.* 42

## 1938 Maserati Tipo 8CTF

## *The Grand Prix Car That Raced Indianapolis*

**IT WAS A BALLED UP MASS OF METAL.** Once proud. Now shattered. The lean, single seat body was rumpled along its length from hitting the wall in turn one, and the great Maserati grille cleanly divided by an infield tree, where the car had finally come to rest. Driver Bud Sennett was unhurt. The year was 1951, the thirty-fifth running of the Indianapolis 500 Mile Race, and the last appearance at Indy for the 1938 Maserati 8CTF. What was a 1938 racecar doing at Indianapolis in 1951? The answer, simply enough, was doing what it had done since 1939, giving the American cars at Indy a run for their money.

### BORN TO RACE

The 3-liter 8CTF Maserati was a car that might never have been were it not for Adolfo Orsi's purchase of the company from the *fratelli Maserati* in 1937. Brothers Ernesto, Ettore, and Bindo remained "privileged" employees, and were given the task of designing and building two new 3-liter Grand Prix cars with which to challenge the Mercedes-Benz W 154 and mighty 12-cylinder German Auto Union D-Types for 1938. The result was the Tipo 8CTF.

Powering the new racecar was a 3-liter straight eight engine made up of two cylinder blocks—the block and head being *tetsa fisa* (one-piece) and mounted on a new bottom end carrying a five plain-bearing crankshaft. The Maserati brothers had essentially doubled the formula from their earlier 1.5-liter design using a Roots-type blower and carburetor duplicated in pairs. The resulting power output of the 8CTF

*Restored to its original color scheme of French Blue with crossed French and American flags on the hood, the first 8CTF, car number 3030, once again bears the Lucy O'Reilly Schell legend and the name of driver René Le Bégue.*

*Powering the 8CTF was a new 3-liter straight eight engine delivering a maximum output of 365 horsepower. Wilber Shaw's car, tuned by master mechanic Cotton Henning for the Indy 500, was limited to 350 horsepower.*

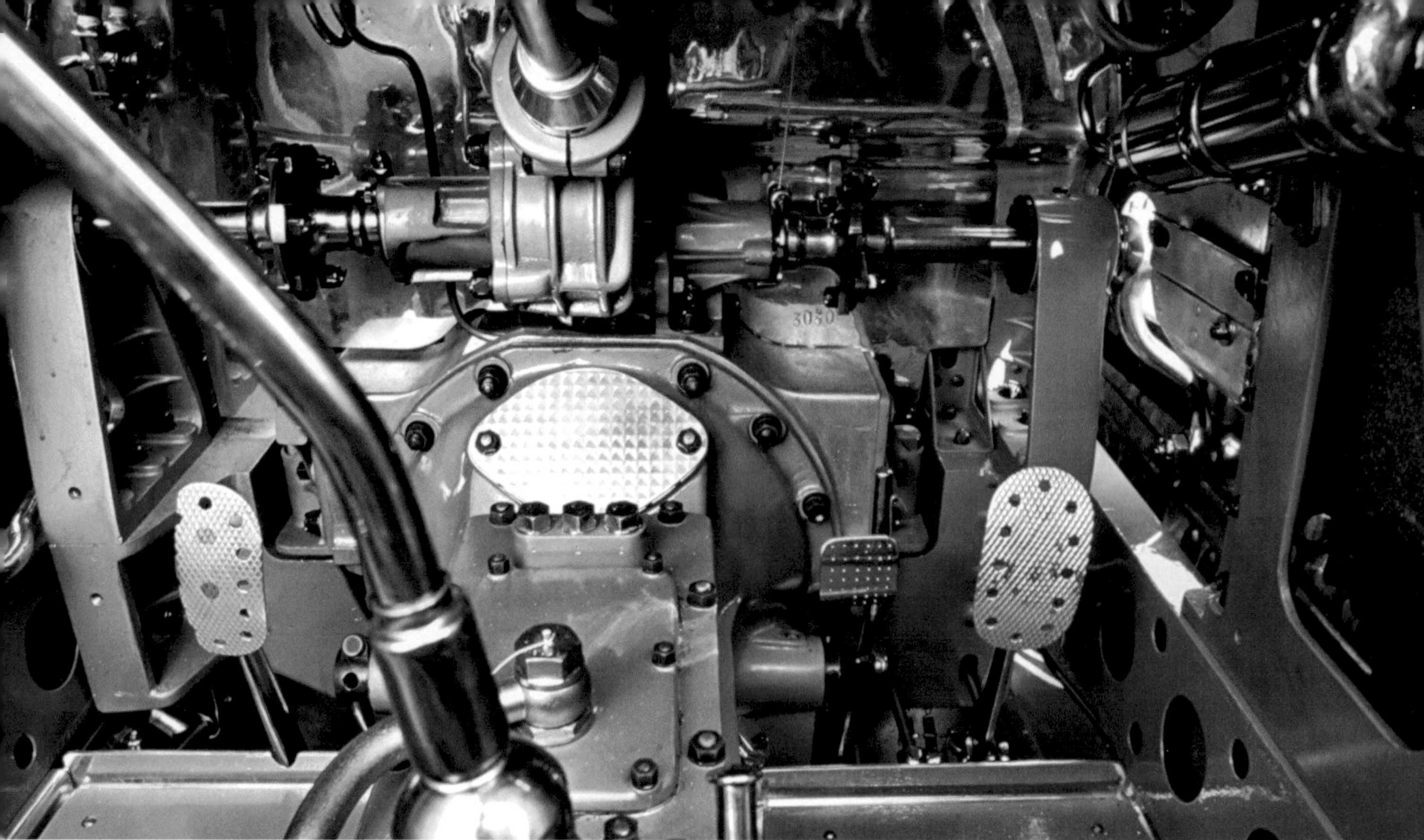

*An all-business cockpit with no comforts, the driver straddled the transmission tunnel with clutch to the left and throttle and brake to the right. The throttle pedal is to the left of the brake pedal!*

was exactly twice that of the 1.5-liter racecar—350 horsepower (later increased to 365) at 6,000 rpm, and promising a speed in top gear of 156 mph.

The first two 8CTF cars, 3030 and 3031, were ready in time for the 1938 Tripoli Grand Prix run on the ferociously fast Mellaha circuit in North Africa. At the wheel were Achille Varzi and celebrated millionaire racecar driver Count Carlo Felice Trossi. Both Maseratis suffered from mechanical problems and withdrew from the race early on, but not before Trossi charged dauntlessly past all three Mercedes entries to take the lead on lap eight. The cars appeared in three Italian races in 1938. At Leghorn, Trossi led the Mercedes again until the engine failed. At Pescara, Luigi Villoresi took over from a weary Trossi, worked up to second place and made fastest lap before the straight eight Maserati engine blew up. At Monza, Trossi drove more conservatively and brought the 8CTF home to a fifth overall finish. For the final 1938 effort, Maserati shipped a car to the Donington Grand Prix in Great Britain, but the gearing was wrong for the race—Luigi Villoresi drove too hard and blew up the engine.

In the United States, Indianapolis Motor Speedway owner Eddie Rickenbacker had changed the rules for the 1938 running of the Indianapolis 500 in order to attract foreign automakers. American Mike Boyle ordered the latest Maserati for Wilbur Shaw to drive but Maserati shipped a 1.5-liter car instead, which Shaw declined to drive. Boyle finally got his 8CTF the following year, car number 3032, complete with an extra 3-liter engine, a box of spare parts, and a selection of Maserati spark plugs.

The car was thoroughly gone over by Boyle's master mechanic Cotton Henning before being handed over to Wilber Shaw. Well aware of the 8CTF's mechanical frailties when driven at the limit, Henning adjusted the superchargers to produce a maximum of 350 horsepower—15 *less* than the factory specifications. This probably saved the engine at Indy.

**THIS IS INDY CAR RACING IN THE FIFTIES, NOTHING BUT A WIND SCREEN BETWEEN YOU AND THE ELEMENTS, THE HEAT OF THE ENGINE AT YOUR FEET, AND THE REVERBERATION OF THE EXHAUST AT YOUR EARS. YOU STRADDLE THE TRANSMISSION TUNNEL WITH THE CLUTCH ON ONE SIDE, THE THROTTLE AND BRAKE ON THE OTHER. YOU NEED TO BE ON YOUR TOES TO DRIVE THE 8CTF, AND TO REMEMBER WHERE YOUR TOES ARE!**

Shaw was immediately taken with the car and found his already estimable skills enhanced by the Maserati's responsive handling. Making full use of the 8CTF's 4-speed gearbox, independent front suspension, and clean, low-drag bodywork, Shaw quickly seized the lead, winning the 1939 race with a two-minute margin, and giving Maserati a decisive and important victory at Indianapolis. It was the first time a European car had won the 500 since Peugeot in 1919. To prove that the Maserati's victory was not luck, Shaw entered the car the following year and won again, leading the 2nd place car by nearly a full lap!

In addition to Shaw's car, in 1940, cars number 3030 and 3031 were campaigned at Indianapolis by the French team of Lucy O'Reilly Schell. The color scheme for the Schell Maseratis was French Blue with crossed French and American flags painted across the hoods. Only one car qualified, composed of teammate René Le Bégue's 8CTF body and frame, number 3030 (the car pictured), fitted with the engine and transmission from René Dreyfus' car number 3031. (Earlier, Dreyfus had blown up the engine in Le Bégue's car during a test run.) Sharing the remaining Maserati, Le Bégue and Dreyfus finished a dismal 10th to Wilber Shaw's rousing second Indianapolis 500 victory with his 8CTF. In 1941, Shaw seemed headed for a hat trick with only 120 miles to go and leading by almost a lap when tire failure denied him his third consecutive victory in the Maserati.

Shaw, who became president of the Indianapolis Motor Speedway after WWII, had more than a passing fancy for the two Maserati 8CTF racecars that returned for the first postwar race in 1946. Number 3030 was entered that year by Frank Brisko as the Elgin Piston Special and driven by Emil Andres. The eight-year-old Maserati managed an impressive 4th place finish, behind Shaw's old Maserati 8CTF being driven by Ted Horn. After several additional runs at Indy, in 1951 Bud Sennett managed to put the now 13-year-old number 3030 Maserati in the race for owner Joe Barzda. It was to be the car's last appearance. The aged 8CTF lost its footing, slid hard into the south wall, and spun off into the infield where it rapped headlong into a tree. This is where our story began.

## PUTTING IT BACK TOGETHER

Years later, repairs were attempted but never successfully completed. The one time it was started the engine promptly put a rod through the block. Racecars, however, are a lot like weeds—unless you completely destroy them, they have a habit of coming back. In the late 1990s, car number 3030 was completely restored at Leydon Restorations in Lahaska, Pennsylvania. The second Schell car, number 3031, went through a 12-year restoration by John Rogers, and the Wilbur Shaw car, number 3032, is still on exhibit at the Indianapolis Motor Speedway Museum. Weeds, indeed. ◆

BONNEVILLE SPECIAL

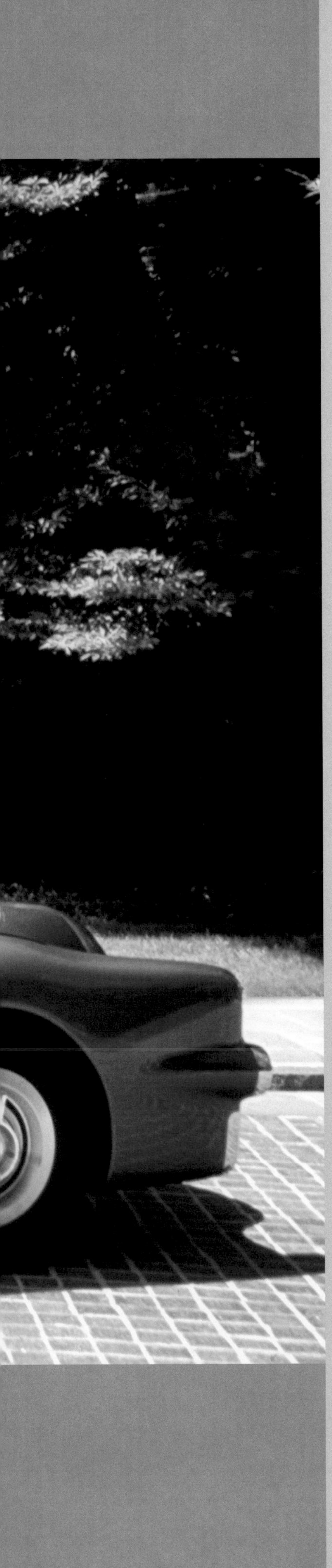

# *No.* 43

## 1954 Pontiac Bonneville Special

### *Perchance to Dream*

**HARLEY EARL'S VISIONS OF THE FUTURE** were often larger than life.

It was the objective of a General Motors Dream Car, such as the 1954 Pontiac Bonneville, to explore the limits of design and to inspire visitors attending the annual GM Motorama to purchase a new car built by one of the Detroit automaker's divisions. The hierarchy established by GM in the 1930s continued well into the postwar era and beyond. Chevrolet was the entry level brand. Above that was Pontiac, then Oldsmobile, Buick, and at the top rung Cadillac. Loyal customers climbed the ladder of ownership throughout their lives, and for the longest time in American automotive history, sons and daughters followed their parents in the choice of an automobile. The Motorama Dream Cars of the 1950s then were the seeds sewn in young impressionable minds, and the visions of a not-too-distant future for their parents.

The Bonneville Special was Pontiac's version of the new 1953 Chevrolet Corvette. GM had determined that the company only needed one sports car, thus Pontiac and Oldsmobile only produced Corvette-styled concept cars. (The F-88 in Oldsmobile's case.)

Harley Earl chose the Bonneville name because it was instantly associated with speed, thanks to the records set by racers at Utah's Bonneville Salt Flats. Inspiration for the design came from Eddie Miller's Pontiac-powered racer, which had set speed records at the Salt Flats in 1950. The first Bonneville Special even wore a special set of Utah license plates issued by the state at the request of Earl.

*A clear Plexiglas top with gullwing-type doors was one of the futuristic features of the Pontiac Bonneville Special Dream Car.*

**The clear canopy gives you a fighter pilot feeling and the interior suggests a Corvette that has been to the chrome factory for an extended stay. It isn't so much about driving the Bonneville Special as it is sitting in it. Turning over the engine and slipping the automatic transmission into "D" is the icing on the cake.**

## MAKING A DREAM COME TRUE

The Bonneville Special was designed by Paul Gillan and Homer LaGassey. They styled the car with only a few features recognizable as Pontiac themes—the silver streaks on the hood and the taillights and their housings. The curves of the front fenders and the recessed headlights bore a resemblance to the Corvette, but other than those familiar features, the low and racy Bonneville Special was unique. A long hood was mandated by the straight eight, followed by a two-passenger cockpit and short rear deck, which resulted in a well-proportioned compact sports car.

Two cars were built, the first painted red-copper with an interior upholstered to match. The second car was metallic green with a green and pewter interior. It differed in a number of features and was a road-ready driver unlike the first car, which was not originally built to be driven. Like the first, both examples managed to survive, even though Motorama cars were supposed to be destroyed after they had served their purpose. Not surprisingly, GM stylists and other company executives found this an unfitting end for their creations and more than a few discreetly went missing or escaped being crushed through the "generosity of strangers."

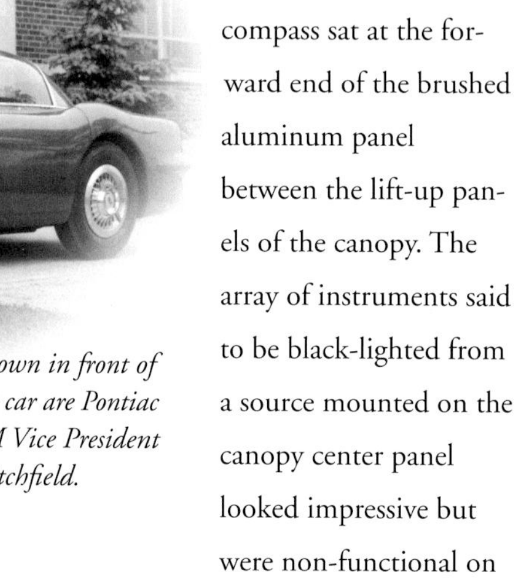

*The 1954 Bonneville Special number one is shown in front of GM's Engineering building. Standing with the car are Pontiac Sales Manager Frank Bridge (at left) and GM Vice President and Pontiac General Manager Robert M. Critchfield. (GM media archive)*

The exterior styling of both Bonneville Specials was exactly what Harley Earl had demanded from the start. The cars stood only 48½ inches high, providing the racy and youthful image Pontiac so desperately needed in the early 1950s to keep pace with other GM divisions.

Inside, the Bonneville Special was an exercise in extreme styling with bucket seats, center console, and instrumentation that included a tachometer. A clock and compass sat at the forward end of the brushed aluminum panel between the lift-up panels of the canopy. The array of instruments said to be black-lighted from a source mounted on the canopy center panel looked impressive but were non-functional on the first car. The second used more conventional gauges that actually worked. Neither car had carpeting. Instead, the floor was finished in brushed aluminum with non-slip rubber strips applied through slots. A competition style, spring-steel, three-spoke

steering wheel along with lap belts and 120-mph speedometer rounded out the racy theme within the Dream Cars. These spectacular experimental models went from the styling team's collective imagination to completed vehicles in only six months!

## THE SURVIVORS

After the national tour ended for each Bonneville Special, the two cars somehow went their separate ways into clandestine ownership. The copper car stayed in storage for several years before it slipped out the door surreptitiously. The second 1954 Bonneville Special was built to tour Pontiac dealerships across the country, though it reportedly made its debut in Los Angeles at the Pan Pacific Auditorium during the GM Motorama tour. Other differences between it and the first car included four air vents in the leading edge of the hood (sans chrome trim), a chrome-plated radiator core support, and a cylinder head painted red instead of being chrome-plated like that of the original.

*The interior of the second Bonneville Special had fully functioning gauges and controls. The floor was finished in brushed aluminum with non-slip rubber strips applied through slots.*

Bonneville Special number two was rumored to have been seriously damaged at the Pontiac dealership in Pontiac, Michigan, and subsequently scrapped. Perhaps there is some truth in the car receiving damage at the dealership, but it was definitely not scrapped! Faithfully restored, it sold on January 21, 2006, at the Barrett-Jackson auction in Scottsdale, Arizona, for $2.8 million plus commission, while designer Homer LaGassey watched the event from the stage. When invited to make a few comments about the metallic green show car, he noted that the Bonneville Special was one of the cars that set the stage for Pontiac's entrance into the youth market in the 1950s and 1960s.[1] ◆

1. *GM's Motorama* by David W. Temple, edited by Dennis Adler, 2006 Motorbooks International.

BUGATTI

# No. 44

## Bugatti Type 51

### The Grand Prix Racecar From Molsheim

**ETTORE BUGATTI BUILT RACECARS AND ROAD CARS.** He was, in many respects, the Enzo Ferrari of the 1920s and 1930s—a constructor, team owner, and manufacturer. Exactly what Enzo, who at the time was working for Alfa Romeo as racing manager, would become after World War II. Bugatti built rugged cars designed for speed, and over the years, from the 1920s to the early 1930s, Bugatti cars won more races than any other.

Bugatti engines were awe-inspiring in their layout and unique in appearance, having squared housings with finely damascened finishes. The logic of this seemingly complicated design was debated for decades. Was it, as some have speculated, Ettore Bugatti's sensitivity to the Cubist Movement of the 1920s that inspired the damascene-finished rectangular shapes? Or, was there a more practical reason for their unique appearance? It is true that Bugatti was born into a family of artists. His father, Carlo, was a sculptor as was Ettore's brother Rembrandt, but in the case of his engines the reason was simplicity. According to Ettore's son Roland, "The Boss (as Ettore was referred to around the factory) did not tolerate the waste of time, labor, or materials. The factory workers were mostly the sons of farmers with few mechanical skills. Slab-sided construction and engine-turned finishes were the most simple." So much for the romance of the Cubist Movement!

*The Type 51 Grand Prix cars were produced from 1931 to 1935. Approximately 40 were built in Type 51 and 51A versions, the latter with a smaller 1.5-liter engine. The cars measured a little over 12 feet in length on a short 95-inch wheelbase. The Type 51 used the same aluminum hoop-spoked wheels pioneered by the Type 35 Grand Prix model. The cars used the traditional front solid axle with the ½ semi-elliptic springs passing through the axle! The solid rear axle was suspended by reverse ¼ elliptical springs.*

## AN IMPROVED MODEL

The Type 51 Bugatti were swift cars suited to virtually any type of road competition. Beneath the hood was one of the most powerful inline eight-cylinder engines of the 1930s, a supercharged 2.3-liter (136.5-cubic-inch) dual overhead cam motor. Based on a Miller design (the head and block), the output was increased by the use of a Roots-type supercharger, which contributed to the Type 51's 160 to 180 horsepower rating at 5,500 rpm. The drive was taken to the rear wheels via a 4-speed gearbox.

The cars were essentially an improved version of Bugatti's celebrated Type 35 Grand Prix cars built from 1924 to 1930.[1] Even with this new model, Ettore held on to long established traditions, including the unique Bugatti front axle design, an artistically striking solid beam confoundingly pierced at its outer corners by semi-elliptic springs passing through the axle shaft! The Bugatti-built gearbox was almost unbreakable, and the massive mechanical brakes adequate to the task of scrubbing off speed until they overheated, the one weakness of most early Bugatti cars. Ettore preferred cable-operated drum brakes and was one of the last automakers to abandon this design.

This example was originally fitted with a Grand Prix body and campaigned by famous French racing driver Louis Chiron, the Michael Schumacher of his era. No other driver has been identified with the brand name Bugatti as closely as Monegasque Chiron. For almost 10 years, he drove for Bugatti in Europe during which he won practically every important championship for the company, including the Grand Prix in Monaco in 1931. After the 1931 season,

1. Bugatti also produced the Type 35B and Type 35 Targa Florio from 1927 to 1930.

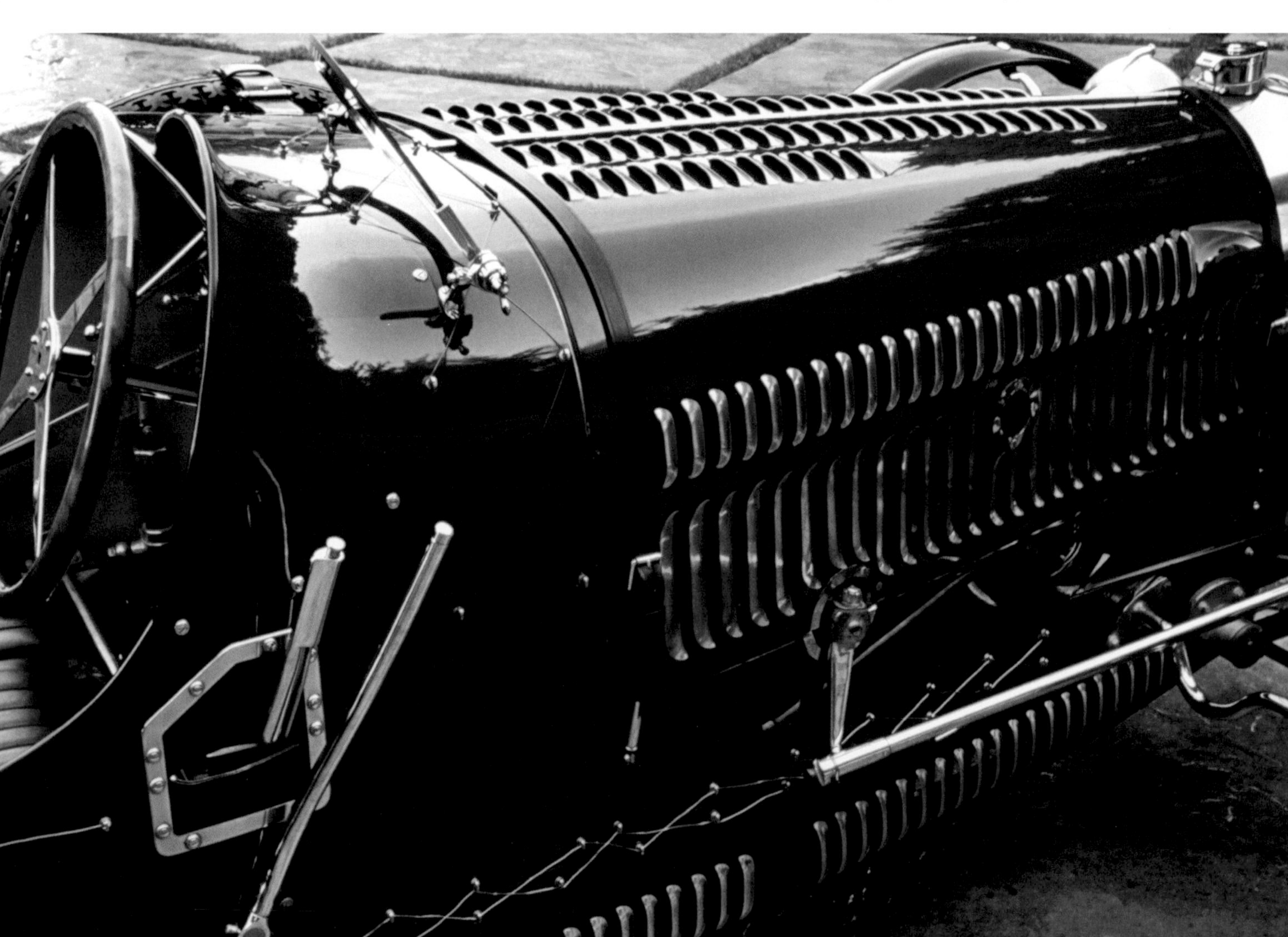

CLAMBER OVER THE SIDE AND INTO THE SEAT, SETTLE IN BEHIND THE HANDSOME WOOD-RIMMED STEERING WHEEL AND PREPARE FOR THE RIDE OF YOUR LIFE. ON A QUIET DAY YOU CAN FIRE UP THE ENGINE ON A TYPE 51 BUGATTI AND LISTEN TO THE ECHO REVERBERATING OFF EVERYTHING FOR HALF A MILE. RUNNING ON TALL TIRES, WITH MECHANICAL BRAKES, THE QUICK RESPONSE OF THE STEERING WILL GIVE YOU A SENSE OF CONFIDENCE, BUT BE CAREFUL HOW YOU DRIVE THIS ONE. IT ONLY GIVES BACK WHAT YOU PUT IN IT.

*Above. The Type 51 interior was that of a traditional Bugatti racecar, gauges only for oil, fuel, and a tachometer. There was no speedometer.*

*Opposite. Wondering where the gear shift was? On the outside along with the hand brake.*

Ettore presented the car to Chiron as a gift. He raced the GP again in 1932 and then sold it.

More than a quarter of a century later the car was purchased by J. B. Nethercutt; however, by then the original Grand Prix body was missing. Mr. Nethercutt had a new one built by Bugatti authority and restorer O. A. Phillips. As shown, the Grand Prix body is set up for road racing and "road equipped" with the addition of fenders, skirts, and windshield, which were removed for Grand Prix competition. One could, and many did, drive Type 35 and Type 51 GP cars on the open road in the 1930s.

The chassis of this car, No. 51133, has actually carried three bodies in its history, the original GP racing body, a sleek aerodynamic coupe body mounted in 1934 or 1935 for the second owner, and the new Grand Prix body built by Phillips in the 1950s. The aerodynamic body, which had been switched to another chassis over half a century ago, was found in 2000 and has since been remounted on its original chassis. The GP body built by Phillips was moved to another Bugatti chassis.

Still a formidable sports car more than 70 years after it was built, a Type 51 Bugatti is capable of speeds reaching 140 mph. Driving in the open cockpit with nothing but an aero screen between you and the elements is a sensation that few modern cars can provide. ◆

# *No.* 45

## 1923 Avions Voisin

### *Valentino's*

**THERE ARE MANY WORDS USED TODAY** to describe star power. In the 1920s there was just one: Valentino. When he arrived, women swooned, men bristled, and cameras flashed. He was a legend, and all that he touched, all that he possessed, became legend as well.

More than 80 years since his last film people still recognize the name. Though the matinee idol who said of himself, "Women are not in love with me but the picture of me on the screen," filmed more than 14 silent epics, he is best remembered by others as one of the great automotive enthusiasts of his time.

In July 1923 he was honeymooning in Paris with his latest wife, set designer Natacha Rambova, who was perhaps the first true love of his life. There they drove virtually every exotic make of car then available, which were made readily accessible to the actor since French sales agents were eager to claim that they had sold a car to the great Valentino. After much deliberation, Rudolph and Natacha decided on a rather obscure marque, a Voisin, and ordered the car fitted with a Victoria Touring body from Parisian *carrossier* J. Rothchild et Fils. It took Rothchild several months to complete the custom body and before it was finished Valentino had returned to America to begin another film.

The Voisin, which cost $14,000 to build, awaited Valentino's return to Europe in 1924, at which time he took delivery and drove it throughout Spain in search of artifacts to use in his next film. (Valentino and his wife spent $100,000 but the film was never made). The car was then shipped back to the United States where he

*The Voisin was painted a pale shade of grey and upholstered in red pleated leather. Although it was designed as a Victoria, Valentino preferred to drive the car in its most informal configuration, as an open tourer.*

*The sporty Voisin carried a removable trunk and dual rear-mounted spare tires.*

proudly drove the handsome Sporting Victoria throughout the streets of Los Angeles, Hollywood, and Beverly Hills for the next two years.

Although his primary residence was in Beverly Hills, Valentino kept the Voisin at his new Hollywood Hills retreat, an eight-acre estate known as Falcon's Lair, which he purchased in 1925. That same year he joined friends Mary Pickford and Douglas Fairbanks at United Artists, earning a salary of $10,000 per week. All seemed well until UA refused to allow his wife, Natacha, to work on any of Valentino's films. The actor stood behind the studio's decision and their romance quickly began to unravel. When Falcon Lair was ready for occupancy, she refused to move in and left for New York. Saddened, Valentino decided to redecorate the house with antiques collected from his films and, behind the wheel of the sporty Voisin, returned to his playboy lifestyle, striking up a romance with Velma Banky, who starred opposite him in *The Eagle*. By the end of the year, Valentino and Banky were a hit in the new film, and his marriage to Natacha had ended in a Paris court. In the settlement, Valentino kept both Falcon Lair and the Voisin, which would remain at the Hollywood Hills estate until his death on August 23, 1926.

## A TOP FOR EVERY MOOD

The Valentino Voisin was unique in several respects, the body having been designed to configure depending upon his mood or the intended purpose of the drive. A traditional Victoria design with a three-position top, allowing either a fully concealed front and rear compartment, an open driver's compartment, or open touring with the fabric completely lowered, there was also a folding rear windscreen for more formal occasions, giving the car the appearance of a dual windshield phaeton. Most often it was driven with the top down and by Valentino alone.

Although the Voisin had a rather stylish aluminum bird sculpture hood ornament designed by the factory, Rudolph Valentino's close friends Douglas Fairbanks and Mary Pickford presented him with a special silver-plated coiled hooded cobra to place atop the Voisin's radiator. The mascot was a gift following the release of the film, *Cobra*. Some say it was a gesture of friendship, others a publicity stunt to promote the movie. Either way, it became one of the most famous hood ornaments of the era. A cobra mascot was also mounted on a Hispano-Suiza found among the cars in Valentino's garage after his death.

The C5 Voisin was an uncommon car, even in France. It was the product of Gabriel Voisin, who had built airplanes from the turn of the century through World War I and had even claimed to have built a practical aeroplane before the Wright Brothers.

When the aircraft business dried up in the post World War I recession, Voisin decided to build automobiles. With a huge factory and 2,000 employees at his disposal, he not only designed and built his own chassis, he produced the engines as well, an almost unbreakable 4-liter, sleeve valve four-cylinder with aluminum pistons (used by Voisin throughout the 1920s), that delivered a robust 90 horsepower and a top speed of 80 mph.

By 1920 more than 1,000 cars had been delivered, and the Voisin quickly become one of the more

*J. Rothchild et Fils designed the Victoria with a folding rear windscreen which was used to give the car a more formal appearance and keep rear seat passengers less buffeted on the open road.*

**THE ENGINE IS QUIET; THE GEARS SHIFT SMOOTHLY IF TREATED RIGHT; AND THE CAR GATHERS SPEED QUICKLY, BUT ITS MASS DEMANDS A COMPETENT HAND AT THE WHEEL. THE VOISIN IS FAST IN THE STRAIGHTAWAY BUT CORNERS LIKE A TRUCK AND REQUIRES DISTANCE TO STOP. AT HEART IT IS A CAR MEANT FOR ARRIVING RATHER THAN GOING. WHEN YOU PULL UP IN A VOISIN, YOU HAVE ARRIVED!**

fashionable automobiles in which to be seen. Much of the credit for that also went to Gabriel Voisin, who had a hand in body designs, which quite often were just short of bizarre, but always interesting. The last Voisin automobiles were built in 1939.

After Valentino's death, an estate auction was held at Falcon Lair and the C5 Voisin was purchased by Robert M. Lawson of Los Angeles. "I kept the car for many years," wrote Lawson in a letter to a later owner. "While it was seldom driven, it was an interesting possession." An apt term. In 1973, the Voisin was purchased from car collector Richard Alexander, and it has been a star in the Nethercutt Museum's Grand Salon ever since. The photographs, incidentally, were taken at Falcon Lair in the exact same place Valentino parked his Avions Voisin in the mid-1920s. ◆

*Valentino (center) was an avid automobilist who liked to work on his cars as well as drive them.*

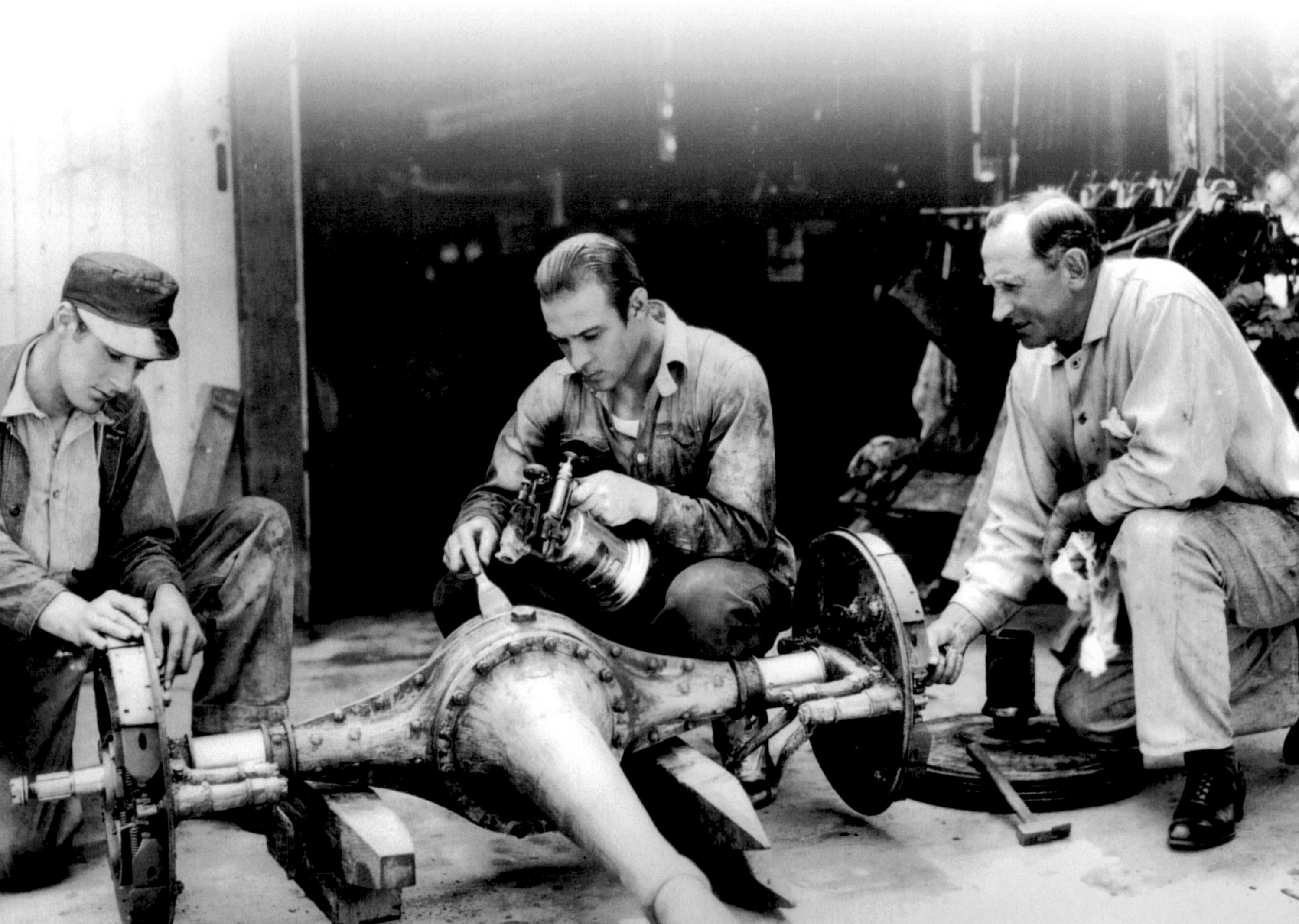

*To promote Valentino's film* Cobra, *some say Douglas Fairbanks and Mary Pickford, the two most powerful actors in Hollywood at the time, made quite a show of presenting Valentino with a hooded cobra radiator mascot for the new Voisin.*

CALIFORNIA
MAYBACH

# No. 46

## 1932 Maybach V12 Zeppelin

### *The Cars Built in Revenge*

**WHILE HISTORY RECOGNIZES GOTTLIEB DAIMLER** and Carl Benz as the two independent automakers who put the world on wheels in the late 1880s, it has always been the work of three men, the third being Wilhelm Maybach, Gottlieb Daimler's closest friend and protégé. Today, when one visits the Daimler-Benz Museum in Untertürkheim, Germany, there are three bronze busts displayed near the entrance, Carl Benz, Gottlieb Daimler, and Wilhelm Maybach. It is mute testimony to the role Maybach played in Mercedes-Benz history. It was he who helped create the first modern car, the 1901 Mercedes, the benchmark against which all other automobiles would be judged for the first decade of the twentieth century. For this effort Maybach was hailed as "King of the Carmakers." The laurels, however, were short-lived.

Following Daimler's death in March 1900, Maybach suddenly found himself in disfavor with the company's board of directors, which had consigned him, along with his son Karl, to heading research and development, a far less important role than Maybach's position as technical director under Gottlieb Daimler. It was a political move to place Daimler's two sons, Paul and Adolf, into management positions within the company. Paul had learned automotive engineering at Maybach's side and the tension continued to grow until 1907, when Maybach resigned from the company he had helped bring into being with Paul's father. With Maybach's departure Paul ascended to the top engineering position at DMG. Younger brother Adolf, who had always been close to Maybach, stepped into the position of factory manager.

*In 1930 the luxurious Maybach 12-cylinder models were renamed Zeppelin in honor of the Maybach-powered airship which flew around the world in 1929.*

The Maybach father and son immediately went to work for Count Ferdinand von Zeppelin and were placed in charge of designing a new aero engine for Zeppelin's giant, lighter-than-air ships. A separate company, which became Maybach Motorenbau Gesellschaft in 1912, was established to produce the Zeppelin engines, and it would be from the M.M.G. factory in Friedrichs-hafen, Germany, that the first Maybach automobiles would emerge following World War I.

## WAR AND PIECES

With Germany out of the aircraft and weapons business, as stipulated in the Treaty of Versailles, the Maybachs turned their attention to auto manufacturing. Some say this was done "in revenge" for the shoddy treatment they had received from Daimler Motors. Ironically, by 1926 Daimler would be forced into a merger of necessity with its biggest competitor, Benz, and the new conglomerate, Daimler-Benz (Mercedes-Benz) would be in direct competition with Maybach for the German luxury and prestige car market by the 1930s.

And while Mercedes were regarded as very stylish, if not sporty automobiles, Maybach maintained a refined, conservative sense of style that appealed to European aristocrats.

HOWEVER LARGE A CAR YOU CAN IMAGINE, A 1930S ERA MAYBACH IS BIGGER. DRIVING A CAR LIKE THIS HANDSOME CABRIOLET, STILL A HUGE AUTOMOBILE, REQUIRES LESS SKILL THAN ATTENTION TO THE ROAD. MAYBACHS SHIFT EASILY, HAVE MORE THAN AMPLE POWER, AND FEEL STEADY ON THE ROAD. MANEUVERING, ON THE OTHER HAND, REQUIRES ROOM. A THREE-POINT TURN BECOMES A SIX-POINT TURN AND IN A MAYBACH, THERE IS NO SUCH THING AS A U-TURN!

Maybach specialized in building limousines, voluminous pullman-cabriolets (seven-passenger convertibles), and four-door cabriolets, most of which were bodied by Karosserie Hermann Spohn in Ravensburg.

While Mercedes was relying on supercharged inline engines in the late 1920s, by 1929, the same year that the airship *Graf Zeppelin* circled the world, powered by five 550-horsepower Maybach V12 engines, Maybach introduced a V12 automobile. This was followed by the 150-horsepower, 7-liter, DS 7 Zeppelin model, and in 1931 the more powerful DS 8, with an 8-liter, 200-horsepower engine. Despite weighing better than three tons, a Zeppelin V12 could easily attain a top speed of 100 mph.

The early V12 models made use of a conventional 3-speed manual transmission with an overdrive unit that allowed six forward speeds. The first DS8 models were equipped with a new 5-speed gearbox design. By 1936, Maybach had introduced a 7-speed gearbox, and a new 5-speed featuring pneumatic operation via two levers on the steering wheel. With the levers set to the correct position, all the driver needed to do to engage a gear was momentarily lift off the accelerator and then depress the throttle again. No declutching was required. The clutch was only used for starting off, stopping, and reversing. The following year, Maybach introduced a 7-speed

*The DS 8 interior was luxuriously appointed, upholstered throughout in supple leather and trimmed in hand-polished burled walnut. The original selling price for the Spohn Cabriolet was $12,000.*

*Delivering a robust 200 horsepower, the Maybach V12 had an immense swept volume of 7,977 cubic centimeters, or about 485 cubic inches. Bore x stroke were 92 mm x 100 mm. Despite most cars weighing more than three tons, a Maybach Zeppelin could easily attain 100 mph.*

with pneumatic shifting that required only one lever on the steering column adjusted from *N* for natural, through top gear and overdrive. Forward and reverse were selected by a separate lever.

## A BEAUTIFUL EXCEPTION

The Maybach DS 8 pictured, which can be seen on display at the Nethercutt Collection Museum in Sylmar, California, was built in 1932 and bodied by Karosserie Spohn as a four-door cabriolet. Although most Maybachs were painted black, befitting their dignified styling, a few coachbuilt models were done in more colorful two-tone paint schemes such as this combination of green and gold.

Approximately 300 Maybach Zeppelins were built between 1930 and 1939. The DS 8 line conferred upon Maybach a stature regarded by the proletariat as closer to that of Rolls-Royce than even the grand Mercedes-Benz 770, an accolade sweeter than revenge.

In the end Daimler and Maybach, as companies, became one. In 1960, the two entered into an agreement whereby Maybach would produce diesel engines for Daimler. The twenty-first century Maybach automobiles, the first to bear the name since 1940, are the most expensive, limited edition models available from Mercedes-Benz. ◆

*No.* 47

# 1933 PACKARD MODEL 1006 V12 SPORT PHAETON

## *The Elegant Open Car*

**AUTOMOTIVE STYLISTS RALPH ROBERTS AND** Raymond Dietrich were responsible for designing a significant number of what we consider today to be classic Packards, particularly Dietrich, who had a way with the subtlety of a body line—its implications and dynamics—quite unlike any other stylist of the era. No one could do so little to a car's appearance yet make so great a difference by changing one line. A *Custom Body By Dietrich* was more than an automobile, it was a signed piece of art.

THE ENGINE OF A PACKARD TWELVE CAN BARELY BE HEARD WHEN IT IS RUNNING. THE TRANSMISSION GLIDES SMOOTHLY THROUGH THE GEARS, AND THE RIDE, THOUGH ROCK SOLID, IS AS COMFORTABLE AS YOUR LIVING ROOM DIVAN. THE DRIVING EXPERIENCE HERE IS IN NOT FEELING LIKE YOU ARE DRIVING, BUT RATHER CRUISING EFFORTLESSLY DOWN THE ROAD IN THE LAP OF LUXURY. THIS CAR BEGS TO BE DRIVEN ALONG THE OLD BLUE HIGHWAYS OF AMERICA.

*Perhaps the greatest of stylist Ray Dietrich's custom body designs for Packard was the 1933 Packard 1006 Sport Phaeton. It featured exquisite exterior styling, a rakishly angled V-frame windshield, rear compartment windscreen, and a sleek profile, even with the top fabric raised.*

In just a few short years, Ray Dietrich had completely revamped Packard's styling and helped create the new semi-custom line, cars that had a noticeably different appearance from Packard's production models but were manufactured in-house rather than by an outside custom coachbuilder. However, the "Packard Individual Customs," designed by Dietrich and coachbuilt in limited numbers, would become the hallmark of his career and the finest examples ever produced under the Packard name.

Among the finest representatives of Dietrich styling were the 1933 Packard 1006 customs, which, aside from having exquisite exterior styling, featured remarkably advanced interior designs for the period, notably, a sweeping dashboard that wrapped around the driving compartment, blending the ends of the instrument panel into the doors. This was accented by Dietrich's rakishly angled V-frame windshields and articulated ventipane fly windows used on dual-windscreen models like the Packard Twelve 1006 Sport Phaeton, a design regarded by many as Ray Dietrich's masterpiece. Only three examples were produced in 1933. The Sport Phaetons were built on the long 147½ inch wheelbase chassis usually reserved for limousines and custom bodies. In general, Phaetons built in 1933 were on the 142-inch 1005 chassis. Although Dietrich fenders and hoods were unique from standard Packard models, the most distinctive characteristic of the Sport Phaetons was the integrated design of the dual windshields, dashboard, and doors.

*It has been called everything from a swan, to a pelican, to a cormorant, but by whatever name, this is the most recognized of all Packard hood ornaments. Packard called it a pelican, introducing the stylish radiator mascot on the 1932 models. Stylized in various renditions throughout the 1930s, 1940s, and 1950s, it remained the Packard symbol until the company's demise in 1957.*

When the first Packard Twelves of the 1930s were delivered (known as the Twin Six in 1932), they boasted an output of 160 horsepower from a 445.5-cubic-inch displacement and were certified to reach 100 mph. Twin Six models, and later Packard Twelves, were accompanied by a *Certificate of Approval* signed by two-time Indy 500 winner (1921 and 1923) Tommy Milton, and Charlie Vincent, director of the Packard Proving Grounds, attesting that the car had been driven 250 miles and conformed, quoting Packard, "to the best Packard standards in acceleration and maximum speed, in control including steering, speed changes and brakes, in roadability and riding qualities, and in all adjustments necessary for . . . all riding and driving conditions."

With their proud, upright grilles, distinguishable from any other car a block away, Packards had a singular, unmistakable style about them, which became a hallmark of the American automotive industry. The 1933 Packard Twelves rank among the greatest cars of the 1930s. ◆

*Above. The body lines were cleaner when the trunk rack was folded up and the optional steamer trunk left at home.*

*Below. Dietrich's unique articulated ventipane rear window for the Sport Phaeton was designed with a channeled arm that rotated the wind wing outward to provide easier entry and exit from the rear seat.*

# No. 48

## 1952 Porsche America

### *Built to Race*

**SOME SAY THAT LEGENDS ARE MADE;** others say that legends are born. We are of the belief that they are indeed made. This one, however, is an obscure legend.

The Porsche America is perhaps the least known of all early 356 models. The lightweight, aluminum-bodied cars were built for racing, and specifically racing in the United States, with the sales of all but one of the cars built handled by American foreign car importer Max Hoffman in New York City.

The America is the true predecessor to the famous 356 Speedster, and true to Porsche racing philosophy, the America had the lowest possible weight, compact dimensions, and very agile handling, making it the ideal sports car with which to challenge the likes of Jaguar, Healey, Allard, and MG in American road racing competition.

More than the rounded "bathtub" styling of the 356 coupes and cabriolets, the America's body design was actually closer to the conventional postwar notion of what a sports car should look like. Some believe Max Hoffman had a hand in dictating the car's styling and modest, but undeniable resemblance to the Jaguar XK-120, which was also being imported by Hoffman at the time. The Americas had a far more graceful, sweeping fender line than the typical 356, cut-down doors, and a rear fender treatment similar to the Jaguar's, although they were unmistakably Porsches when seen from the front and rear.

*Introduced in 1952, only 16 Porsche America Roadsters were built. Intended for sale in the United States, all but one was sold by New York City importer Max Hoffman. (John Paterek collection)*

WROTE RACER AND AUTHOR JOHN BENTLEY: "IN THE MATTER OF HANDLING THE ROADSTER IS NEITHER MORE NOR LESS SENSITIVE THAN THE OTHER MODELS. THE REDUCED WEIGHT ENHANCES ITS EXCELLENT ROADABILITY, PROVIDED YOU OBSERVE THE SAME BASIC PRECAUTIONS AS WITH ANY OTHER PORSCHE. THAT IS, ALWAYS GET YOUR BRAKING AND SHIFTING OVER AND DONE WITH BEFORE YOU ENTER A CORNER, AND GO THROUGH UNDER MODERATE POWER, WISHING (RATHER THAN STEERING) THE CAR AROUND."

The frame was taken from the 356 Cabriolet but fitted with an aluminum roadster's body. Equipped with Porsche's new 75-horsepower 1500S engine, the America weighed just 1,580 pounds. There were no frills in the cockpit. For storage there was an open cubbyhole in the dashboard and hollows in the doors. Instead of roll-up windows, drop-in plastic side curtains were used.

Intended for both road and track, the America could easily be stripped down for competition by removing the windshield and replacing it with the curved plastic aeroscreen that came with the car. The manually folded canvas top was simply sprung into

*The interior of the America was simple. No roll-up windows, only necessary instruments, and hollows in the doors and dashboard for storage. Note the upright shift lever. Many of the early Porsche parts came from VW.*

*The small, 1,580-pound sports car was intended for American sports car club racing. Author and racecar driver John Bentley recorded a top speed of 110 mph in 1953.*

place by two pins and easily removed; even the bumpers could be unbolted in a matter of minutes. By additionally removing the baggage compartment, jack, tool kit, and wheel covers, the weight of the car could be reduced by more than 100 pounds. That made a big difference on the track—a stripped down America could easily overtake a more powerful Jaguar XK-120 as well as out-corner and out-brake anything anywhere near its $4,600 price in the genuine sports car line. At the inaugural SCCA (Sports Car Club of America) race weekend in Thompson, Connecticut, in the fall of 1952, Hoffman had three Porsche America Roadsters on the track for the 1500cc class race. The America's legend was made in a day. *Auto Age* editor and racecar driver John Bentley was the owner of the first America Roadster built, which he purchased from American sportsman Briggs S. Cunningham in 1953.

In his road test, Bentley's America accelerated to 60 mph in 9.3 seconds, covered the standing quarter-mile in 17.9 seconds and reached a maximum speed of 110 mph. In 1953, for a four-cylinder car, that was heroic!

Production of the America Roadster was limited to 16 cars; all but one were sold in the United States by Max Hoffman. ◆

# No. 49

## 1952 Nash-Healey

### *American, British, and Italian Ingenuity*

**WHAT EXACTLY IS A SPORTS CAR?** The answer depends on when you're asking the question. In the early 1900s it was best defined as a runabout: a chassis with two seats, a hood over the engine, a copious fuel tank, and maybe some fenders. In the 1920s it could have been a Kissel Gold Bug Speedster (in fact it was), in the 1930s an SSJ Duesenberg. But when we ask the same question in the early

DRIVING A NASH-HEALEY IS DIFFERENT THAN A TYPICAL AMERICAN CAR OF THE 1950S. IT COMES VERY CLOSE TO THE BRITISH IDEAL OF A SPORTS CAR. YOU CAN FLING IT INTO A CORNER AND MANHANDLE IT THROUGH OR SIMPLY LET THE ROAD TAKE YOU AWAY AND MOTOR ALONG WITHOUT A CARE IN THE WORLD.

1950s, the answer is quite different. In modern day terms, America didn't have a production sports car until 1951, when Nash president George Mason got together with British sports car legend Donald Healey and Italian stylist Sergio "Pinin" Farina.

In the 1950s, Sergio "Pinin" Farina (the family name was still Farina at this point in time) would become the first Italian to design cars for American automakers, and

*The Nash-Healey was America's first postwar production sports car. With a 140-horsepower, six-cylinder engine, it was fast enough to win its class at Le Mans in 1952 and finish 3rd overall in the 24-hours. (Al Ruckey collection)*

*Pinin Farina's design for the Nash-Healey created a striking profile, measuring 175.75 inches from bumper to bumper. Pinin Farina's eye-catching lower door line, which swept up into the rear fenders, was copied by Mercedes-Benz stylists two years later on the 1954 model 190 SL roadster.*

that included America's first postwar sports car, the magnificent 1951 Nash-Healey. The car's chassis and suspension were engineered in England by Donald Healey, with the body designed and built in Italy by Carrozzeria Pinin Farina, while power for this international concoction came from Kenosha, Wisconsin, automaker Nash.

Unlike in Europe, where sports cars were an everyday sight, in the United States they were still more of a curiosity after World War II. In fact, in 1952 a total of 11,199 new sports cars were registered in the United States. This amounted to an insignificant 0.27 percent of car registrations for the year! Among that total were a handful of Nash-Healy two-seaters powered by Nash six-cylinder engines that had been "tweaked" by Donald Healey to produce 125 horsepower. As production continued in 1952, the engine was bored an eighth of an inch, raising swept volume to 252.6 cubic inches and output to 140 horsepower.

The hallmark of all Donald Healey cars was speed and agility. The Nash-Healey established itself with sports car enthusiasts by winning the "3001-5000cc Class" at the 1952 Le Mans 24-hour marathon, and placing 3rd overall behind a pair of more powerful and purpose-built Mercedes. Even more significant, the Nash-Healey had also beaten Ferrari, Aston Martin, Jaguar, and Talbot-Lago sports cars at the Circuit de la Sarthe. Following the racing success in France, Nash launched a national advertising campaign that cost the automaker, according to Donald Healey, more than the entire investment in the Nash-Healey project! The company even hung the Le Mans label on the Ambassador and Statesman sedans (also designed by Pinin Farina) when equipped with the dual-barrel "power pack" carburetor used in the Le Mans-winning Nash-Healey.

Sold exclusively through Nash dealerships across the country, the Nash-Healey made its United States debut in February 1952 at the Chicago Automobile Show and became America's first production postwar sports car, beating the Corvette to market by a full year. Ironically, with success at its doorstep, Nash began to back away from the sporty two-seater by 1953. Mason had never intended for the car to be a high-volume model. Production peaked that year with a total of 162 cars, and between 1952 and 1954, only 506 were built. When Nash merged with Hudson in 1954, creating American Motors Corporation (AMC), there was no place in the newly combined product line for a sports car. The Nash-Healey, one of the truly great postwar cars, was gone in 1955. But for the sports car enthusiast of the twenty-first century, riding in a Nash-Healey is a definite must. ◆

*The Italian-inspired sporty lines of the Nash-Healey were offset by the Nash grille and headlights, which closely resembled the Nash Ambassador and Statesman.*

United

# No. 50

## 1958 Buick Century Caballero Estate Wagon

### *Chrome by the Ton*

**THE 1959 CADILLAC ELDORADO MAY BE THE ICON** of an era, but drive down the street in this car and every head will turn. And yes, it is a station wagon.

Aside from the Eldorado, the most ostentatious set of wheels on the American road in the late 1950s belonged to the Buick Century Caballero Estate Wagon. It

THIS IS THE IMAGE OF THE FIFTIES, WHEN OSTENTATIOUS WAS A STYLING CUE AND GOOD TASTE HAD NOTHING TO DO WITH AUTOMOTIVE DESIGN. FROM BEHIND THE WHEEL OF A CENTURY CABALLERO ESTATE WAGON YOU WILL COMMAND MORE ATTENTION FROM OTHER DRIVERS, NEIGHBORS, AND PEOPLE WHO HARDLY EVER NOTICE CARS THAN YOU WILL IN A BRAND NEW FERRARI.

embodied every styling cliché that Detroit designers had conceived since chrome and fins crawled out of the primordial ooze. The Buick's massive "Fashion-Aire Dynastar" grille opened up like a lascivious grin with 160 chromed squares, each of

*At nearly 18 feet in length the Caballero provided all the comforts of home and nearly as much square footage. Buick produced 4,456 Buick Century Caballero Estate Wagons, of which only a handful remain today. It is a far more rare car than a 1959 Cadillac Eldorado. (Randy Mytar collection. DC-3 courtesy Clay Lacy Aviation)*

*The last of their kind, the 1958 Buicks were a high water-mark in outrageous styling.*

them with four triangular surfaces to reflect light, bordered by chromed bullet parking lights and a Cadillac-style lower bumper supporting two large conical grille guards. And that's just the front end.

The Estate Wagon, Buick's upscale name for what everyone else called a station wagon, was the ultimate family car: four doors, two immense bench seats, and a rear cargo floor the size of a Nash Metropolitan. The cars did have their more refined points, with very stylish cut-down front doors, and a pillarless design that gave the Estate Wagon a stunning profile. And now back to the chrome.

Buick's chrome obsession continued with "Vista Vision" dual headlights topped with chrome-edged brows that continued down the side of the car into a bold "sweepspear" running to the rear-wheel opening. From there it continued over the wheel arches to the rear bumper capped at either end by massive chromed guards. Not to be outdone by the bumpers, the rear quarter panels were accented with chromed louvers and 10 speed lines leading back to tall, chrome-draped tailfins. Not surprisingly, the Caballero Estate Wagon weighed more than 4,500 pounds.

To move two-and-a-half tons of automobile, Buick placed a 300-horsepower, 364-cubic-inch V8 under the hood with Quadrajet carburetors and a heavy breathing 10.0:1 compression ratio. One thing the big Buick could do really well was go fast.

Buick's great transgression in chrome only appeared for the 1958 model year, the mantle for excess thence being passed on to the new Cadillac Eldorado in 1959. But for one year, the Buick Century Caballero Estate Wagon was your father's dream car and your worst nightmare: a six-passenger wagon ready for all those family road trips—just mom, dad, sissy, and you—heading off for the great out-of-doors. Yessireebob—sing-a-longs, greasy roadside diners, Burma Shave signs, winding mountain roads, and of course, car sickness. A ride in a Caballero is a ride back to the good old days. ◆

*Above. The Caballero Estate Wagon weighed more than 4,500 pounds. To move two-and-a-half tons of automobile, Buick placed a 300-horsepower, 364-cubic-inch V8 under the hood with Quadrajet carburetors and a heavy breathing 10.0:1 compression ratio.*

*Below. Interiors were offered in a choice of distinctively patterned Cordaveen in two-tone green, two-tone blue, red and white, black and white, tan and beige, plus a rust cloth with beige bolsters. Buick also offered padded dashboards as a safety feature.*

# Appendix

## 50 Must-see Car Museums

*Compiled by West Peterson*

This is a comprehensive list of "open-to-the-public" museums. Before setting out to visit any of them, it is very important that you call to understand their hours of operation and the days in which they are open. Many are closed on certain days of the week and some are closed during certain times of the year.

### ALABAMA

International Motorsports Hall of Fame
P.O. Box 1018
Talladega, AL 35160
(256) 362-5002
www.motorsportshalloffame.com

Mercedes-Benz Visitor's Center Museum
1 Mercedes Dr.
Tuscaloosa, AL 35490
(205) 507-2252
www.mbusi.com

### ARIZONA

Franklin Automobile Museum
1405 E. Kleindale Rd.
Tucson, AZ 85719
(520) 326-8038
www.franklinmuseum.org

### CALIFORNIA

Blackhawk Museum
3700 Blackhawk Plaza Circle
Danville, CA 94506
(925) 736-2280
www.blackhawkmuseum.org

Deer Park Auto Museum
29013 Champagne Blvd.
Escondido, CA 92026
(760) 749-1666

Lucas Automotive Museum
2850 Temple Ave.
Long Beach, CA 90806
(800) 952-4333

Marconi Automotive Museum for Kids
1302 Industrial Dr.
Tustin, CA 92680
(714) 258-3001
www.marconimuseum.org

Nethercutt Collection/San Sylmar
15180 Bledsoe St.
Sylmar, CA 91342
(818) 367-2251
www.nethercuttcollection.org

Petersen Automotive Museum
6060 Wilshire Blvd.
Los Angeles, CA 90036
(323) 930-2277
www.petersen.org

San Diego Automotive Museum
2080 Pan American Plaza
San Diego, CA 92101
(619) 231-2886
www.sdautomuseum.org

Towe Auto Museum
2200 Front St.
Sacramento, CA 95818
(916) 442-6802
www.toweautomuseum.org

### COLORADO

Cussler Museum
14959 West 69th Ave.
Arvada, CO 80007
(303) 420-2795
www.cusslermuseum.com

Forney Transportation Museum
4303 Brighton Blvd.
Denver, CO 80216
(303) 297-1113
www.forneymuseum.com

Shelby American Collection
5020 Chaparral Ct.
Boulder, CO 80308

(303) 516-9565
www.shelbyamericancollection.org

## DELAWARE

Friends of Auburn Heights Preserve
3000 Creek Rd.
Yorklyn, DE 19726
(302) 239-2385
www.auburnheights.org

## FLORIDA

Don Garlits Museum
13700 SW 16th Ave.
Ocala, FL 34473
(877) 271-3278
www.garlits.com

Tallahassee Antique Car Museum
3550A Mahan Dr.
Tallahassee, FL 32308
(850) 942-0137
www.tacm.com

Tampa Bay Automobile Museum
3301 Gateway Centre Blvd.
Pinellas Park, FL 33782
(727) 579-8226
www.tbauto.org

## GEORGIA

Bruce Weiner Microcar Museum
2950 Eaton Rd.
Madison, GA 30650
(706) 343-9937
www.microcarmuseum.com

Stone Mountain Car & Treasure Museum
Robert E. Lee Blvd.
Stone Mountain, GA 30083
(770) 413-5229
www.stonemountainpark.com

## ILLINOIS

Museum of Science and Industry
57th St. and Lake Shore Dr.
Chicago, IL 60637
(773) 684-1414
www.msichicago.org

## INDIANA

Auburn Cord Duesenberg Museum
1600 South Wayne St.
Auburn, IN 46706
(260) 925-1444
www.acdmuseum.org

Indianapolis Motor Speedway Museum
4790 West 16th St.
Indianapolis. IN 46224
(317) 492-6784
www.indianapolismotorspeedway.com

Kruse Auto & Carriage Museum
5634 County Rd. 11-A
Auburn, IN 46706
(260) 927-9144
www.kccmuseum.org

National Auto & Truck Museum—NATMUS
US 1000 Gordon M. Buehrig Place
Auburn, IN 46706
(260) 925-9100
www.natmus.com

Studebaker National Museum
201 S. Chapin St.
South Bend, IN 46601
(574) 235-9714
www.studebakermuseum.org

## KENTUCKY

National Corvette Museum
350 Corvette Dr.
Bowling Green, KY 42101
(270) 781-7973
www.corvettemuseum.com

## MAINE

Owls Head Transportation Museum
117 Museum St.
Owls Head, ME 04854
(207) 594-4418
www.ohtm.org

Seal Cove Auto Museum
20 Mechanic St.
Camden, ME 04843
(207) 244-9242
www.sealcoveautomuseum.org

Stanley Museum
40 School St.
PO Box 77
Kingfield, ME 04947
(207) 265-2729
www.stanleymuseum.org

## MASSACHUSETTS

Larz Anderson Auto Museum
The Museum of Transportation
15 Newton St.
Brookline, MA 02445
(617) 522-6547
www.mot.org

Heritage Museum and Gardens
67 Grove St.
Sandwich, MA 02563
(508) 888-3300
www.heritagemuseumsandgardens.org

## MICHIGAN

Alfred P. Sloan Museum
1221 E. Kearsley St.
Flint, MI 48503
(810) 237-3453
www.sloanmuseum.com

Gilmore Car Museum
6865 Hickory Rd.
Hickory Corners, MI 49060
(269) 671-5089
www.gilmorecarmuseum.org

Henry Ford Museum and
Greenfield Village
20900 Oakwood Blvd.
Dearborn, MI 48121
(313) 271-1620
(313) 982-6001
www.hfmgv.org

Walter P. Chrysler Museum
One Chrysler Dr.
Auburn Hills, MI 48326
(248) 944-0001
www.chryslerheritage.com

Ypsilanti Auto Heritage Museum
100 East Cross St.
Yspilanti, MI 48198
(734) 482-5200
www.ypsiautoheritage.org

## MISSOURI

'57 Heaven
1600 W. Hwy. 76
Branson, MO
(417) 332-1957
www.57heaven.com

## NEVADA

Imperial Palace Auto Collection
3535 Las Vegas Blvd. S.
Las Vegas, NV 89109
(702) 794-3174
www.autocollections.com

National Automobile
Museum/Harrah
10 Lake Street S.
Reno, NV 89501
(775) 333-9300
www.automuseum.org

## NEW YORK

Buffalo Transportation Museum
263 Michigan Ave.
Buffalo, NY 14203
(716) 853-0084
www.pierce-arrow.com

## OHIO

Citizen's Motorcar Co. (Packard)
420 South Ludlow St.
Dayton, OH 45402
(937) 226-1710
www.americaspackardmuseum.org

Crawford Auto/Aviation Museum
10825 East Blvd.
Cleveland, OH 44106
(216) 721-5722
www.wrhs.org/crawford

## PENNSYLVANIA

AACA Antique Auto Museum
161 Museum Dr.
Hershey, PA 17033
(717) 566-7100
www.aacamuseum.org

William E. Swigart, Jr. Auto
Museum
Route 22
Huntingdon, PA 16652
(814) 643-0885
www.swigartmuseum.com

## TENNESSEE

Floyd Garrett Musclecar Museum
320 Winfield Dunn Pkwy.
Sevierville, TN 37876
(865) 908-0882
www.musclecarmuseum.com

Lane Motor Museum
702 Murfreesboro Pike
Nashville, TN 37210
(615) 742 7445
www.lanemotormuseum.org

## TEXAS

Pate Museum of Transportation
18501 Hwy 377 S.
Ft. Worth, TX
817-332-1161
www.texasescapes.com/FortWorth
Texas/Pate-Museum-of-
Transportation.htm

## WASHINGTON

LeMay Museum/America's Car
Museum
325 152nd St. E.
Tacoma, WA 98445
(253) 536-2885
www.lemaymuseum.org

## WISCONSIN

Wisconsin Automotive Museum
147 N Rural St.
Hartford, WI 53027
(262) 673-7999
www.wisconsinautomuseum.com

West Peterson is editor of the *Antique Automobile,* the official publication of the Antique Automobile Club of America, the nation's oldest and largest old car society, established in 1935.